Also by Dale Dauten

The Gifted Boss
The Max Strategy

The
Laughing Warriors

How to Enjoy Killing the Status Quo

By
Dale Dauten

Lumina Media

Book design by Jim Camp and Mark Cashion

Jacket design by Ryan Kelly

ISBN: 1-4392-4681-5

www.dauten.com

10 9 8 7 6 5 4 3 2 1

To Joel and Jeri,
who taught me
Make yourself useful.

History repeats itself.
That's one of the things wrong with history.

— Clarence Darrow

You can lead a horse to water, but if you can get it to float on its back
you've got something.

— Conrad Schneiker

The Second Day

(very loosely adapted from a thirteenth-century
Zen story by the Japanese teacher Muju)

On a mountain estate, overlooking the sea, lives a woman raised among the Samurai. In her youth, she was so crafty a warrior that legend claimed she could fly and disappear. As she aged, she turned her energies away from the dragons of war, instead confronting those of the marketplace, building a manufacturing company renowned throughout Asia for the efficiency of its good-hearted workers.

One day a young merchant came to The Wise One and appealed for her counsel. He explained that the workers he employed were small-minded and demanding, as were the owners who employed him. He begged her to enlighten him, to show him The Way.

"In the past month," she asked him, "what have you learned about working?" To his halting response, she smiled and said, "If you aren't learning, you're not doing it right." She added, "Come back to me in six months and report your progress." Then she stood and walked from the room.

For six months the young man studied. When he went back to The Wise One he told her with strained voice, "I have read every book I could buy or borrow. I prevailed upon my cousin in America to send me books written by its famous business philosophers, Covey and Drucker. How I labored! Their writings were like a great river—deep and slow. Yet I did not falter. I instructed one of my assistants to stand by my side as I read and to strike me with a bamboo stick when I started to fall asleep. Yet, for all my suffering, I have not learned The Way."

The woman smiled and said this about his work: "If you're not laughing, you're

1

not doing it right." Again she instructed him to report to her in six months.

He returned a gloomy man, telling stories of hiring jugglers and magicians and walking about forcing himself to chuckle. "I even learned to make balloon animals to entertain the workers—it made me feel foolish and inspired the workers to look upon me with pity."

The Wise One abruptly turned toward the massive doors that were open to the courtyard. An owl flew in, landed on the chair beside her, and seemed to speak to her. When she turned back to the young merchant, she confided with soft compassion, "I have just been told that you have only three days. If you have not found The Way in three days, you will die. There are no alternatives, no appeals. I am sorry."

On the second day, the young merchant found The Way.

* * *

In the fashion of Zen stories, this one ends abruptly, leaving the reader to ponder the story's moral. What the merchant learned on the second day took me into my second decade of research and writing. The pages that follow are a collection of examples of business at its best. You'll meet some of the wisest and most interesting people I located in twenty years of searching for those who are learning, laughing, and getting it right. At the end of the book, we'll return to our young merchant and discover his revelation about the human nature of achievement. I'll try to get us there quickly—before you have need of an assistant with a bamboo stick.

PART ONE
LAUGHING WARRIORS
AND
THE ART OF CREATIVE USEFULNESS

- *Think like a hero: Who can I help today?*
- *Work like an artist: What else can we try?*
- *Refuse to be ordinary: Pursue excellence, then kill it.*
- *Celebrate, but take no credit.*

Introduction

Samurai about to enter battle would call out to the enemy their names, ranks, and accomplishments. This was not boasting; it was meant to bring forth a worthy opponent and thus the possibility of an honorable victory.

Most people in modern organizations devote their lives to fighting unworthy opponents, to a dreary battle-of-attrition with small troubles. Further, most leadership is really just revised following, consisting of replacement role models to imitate. Thus, most workdays amount to a slow run in tight shoes.

However, when a group of minds are together charmed by a "better way" problem, then work stops being drudgery and starts being magic, for that's when customers, employees, and suppliers come together to help one another.

As we shall see, worthy problems require "creative usefulness," which brings a warrior spirit to innovative helping. The samurai of the modern organization aren't just fighting deadlines or bureaucracy or even the competition; they are searching out better ways to serve, while faced off against the current standard of quality. The goal of the warrior is this: Identify and pursue the highest level of the status quo, then kill it. In other words; pursue excellence, then kill it.

Send in the Dragons

What's a hero without a nemesis? The more evil the villain, the more celebrated the hero. No more small victories; bring on the dragons.

THE VIEW FROM THE MOUNTAIN OF DRAGONS

– If you're out of work, you've got problems.

– So you get a job, and with it you get a boss—which means, of course, management problems.

– Get to be the boss, and then you get employee problems.

– Solve your employee problems, and you have people who bring in customers . . . and customer problems.

– Overcome your customer problems, then you're growing so fast you get supply problems.

– Resolve your supply problems, and you'll expand so rapidly that you encounter cash flow problems.

– Surmount financial obstacles, and you're such a business success that you attract imitators, and, with them, competitor problems.

– Figure out how to overcome competitor problems, then you're a monopoly and . . .

Stop and enjoy the view from the top of the Mountain of Dragons: antitrust problems.

The "Chi" of Organizations

Where do leaders and other high achievers find the strength and motivation to engage zestfully in the battle with the dragons of the status quo?

There is a point at which work passes into emotion, where it manufactures energy rather than drains it. Business at its best is about emotion. While most business and consumer decisions seem to be rational, that's just a front. We are emotional beings pretending to be rational.

The Asian cultures have an advanced understanding of energy flows, as evidenced by acupuncture, tai chi and feng shui. I believe there is need for a similar appreciation of the life force of organizations. When the organizational "chi"—"life force" or "spirit"—gets blocked, Laughing Warriors employ the acupuncture of curiosity and service.

In preparation for speaking to a President's Club of top sales reps for a major telecommunications company, I chatted with some of the company's sales managers, inviting their thoughts on what made their best reps so successful. A few themes emerged: The star sales reps are, according to their managers, persistent, goal oriented, numbers driven, and, above all, they maintain a positive attitude. Nothing new there. Then it got interesting.

I sent a questionnaire to the people attending the meeting, inquiring about their work, including their best sale and their personal "trademark." My goal was to find some stories to colorfully illustrate what the sales managers had said. It didn't happen. Out of nearly 150 sales stars talking about their work, just one mentioned persistence; only a handful spoke of their goals or of a numbers orientation; and, likewise, only a few spoke of their attitude.

So I reread their answers looking for a new pattern, whereupon I immediately saw that the top sales people were NOT focused on their own attitudes, but on those of their customers. The top reps spoke of getting customers to smile and laugh, and described how they wanted customers to feel, especially to feel helped. There was also a theme of pride in their abilities, both to save their clients money or time and to resolve problems.

As I compared what the sales managers had told me to what the top reps had actually said, I realized that I was looking at…

The Old Language of Success—
Persistence, Goals, Numbers, Positive Attitude;
Versus
The New Language of Success—
Smiling, Laughing, Feelings, Saving, Helping.

This new language isn't just spoken by sales reps for one major company. As I've talked to the most admirable people in every profession, they're all in the same business: helping.

Some people associate "helping" with being subservient and meek. However, when it comes to top performers, helping isn't just being nice. It's something far sturdier—the old expression "stouthearted" comes to mind. And while it takes humility to be a helper, high achievers don't seem meek or humble; in fact, they seem like warriors, ones who laugh a lot. So what do they know that less successful helpers don't?

In his book *Good to Great*, Jim Collins describes his surprise at finding that the leaders of great companies were routinely described as "quiet," "reserved," "self-effacing" and "modest." This was in contrast to executives in lesser companies whom he described as having a "very I-centric style." Most people share Collins's surprise; after all, most people know executives from what they see on television, and generalizing about executives from television is like generalizing about zoologists from watching "Crocodile Hunter." We mostly see the executives who choose to be visible, while most gifted bosses are preoccupied with their work rather than their public image. Collins writes, "It's not that [the leaders of great companies] have no ego or self-interest. Indeed, they are incredibly ambitious—but their ambition is first and foremost for the institution, not themselves."

Collins stopped short: it's ambitious helpfulness that motivates the best bosses and the best employees; it's not just growth for the sake of growing an institution, but growth for the sake of growing usefulness, which means figuring out how to be different and better at helping customers.

To Defeat vs. To Enrich

Robert Thurman (wise man, professor at Columbia University, first Westerner to be recognized by the Dalai Lama as a Tibetan Buddhist monk, and, by the way, father to the actress Uma Thurman) said in a speech, "One of the lies of the machinery of unenlightenment is that you are meaningless. Everything we do resonates infinitely, for good or ill. Every moment hinges into eternity."

Well, if every moment hinges into eternity, then what does that imply for how most of us spend most of our minutes, at work? After hearing Thurman speak, I arranged an interview with him to explore how business and work fit into the enlightened life he describes. That's when Thurman offered this description of history: "Buddhism is closely allied to the merchant class and was part of the shift of power from military to merchant. Business, in the proper spirit, results in both sides—buyer and seller—becoming enriched; whereas in the military, one side wins and one loses. We're still trying to accomplish that transition."

As I visit organizations, I find they can be arranged on a continuum from "Organized to Defeat" to "Organized to Enrich." It struck me that this would apply not just to transactions but to dealings with employees as well. Thurman agreed, saying, "The latest medical research is saying that the quantity of the work you do is not a risk factor. They used to think that being a workaholic was unhealthy. But the important factor is if you like your work. It isn't doing a lot of work that's dangerous, it's doing a lot of work that you hate." But it struck me that finding enjoyable work was simpler than finding some job that would contribute to Thurman's definition of the highest level of existence: "A being who has fallen in love with all beings and can see in them their future perfection."

He said gently, "Work is something we humans like to do. Even when the product seems mundane or unromantic, you still have to relate to people, so you have the opportunity to make it wonderful. You have the chance to develop friendships. The product could be mundane, but that doesn't mean the relationships have to be of lesser quality. And that makes work spiritual."

Just before we ended our conversation, Thurman asked me about my work on this book. To my response he made a humming sound, then said merrily: "Ah, then you have a great obligation to uplift people."

Later, as I contemplated that sweet-natured imperative, "the obligation to uplift," it stuck me that the phrase made a rousing job description, one that would fit anyone who wants to be part of organization built around enriching rather than defeating.

The New Warriors of Enrichment

Paramahansa Yogananda (a philosophical brother to the Dalai Lama) once advised, "Meet everybody on the battlefield of life with the courage of a hero and the smile of a conqueror." There's something about that image of a "smiling conqueror" that fits people like Robert Thurman and other admirable achievers. They have warrior energy directed to enriching the lives of others. They stride over "the battlefield of life" looking for dragons of complacency and mediocrity.

These modern warriors of enrichment employ a weapon that seems superhuman because it's unseen and misunderstood and therefore mystical. They have learned to dip into the river of energy that arises from the best of human nature and, thus, the best of themselves. Doing so, they are practitioners of The Way of Creative Usefulness. This allows work to be lifted from mere employment to spiritual endeavor.

Although I don't often see religion in enlightened workplaces, I do see spirituality in the people working there. This calls to mind Carl Jung, who said, "Bidden or unbidden, God is present." Dr. Larry Dossey, a physician fascinated by the studies that show that prayer affects healing, brought together more than a hundred studies on the effects of prayer. One of the results he noted was that patients who are prayed for (even when they don't know of the prayers) heal significantly faster than those in a control group. These are controlled experiments, "hard" data. No wonder nearly half of doctors pray for their patients.

Dossey has a line in his book, a saying of Jewish mystics, "Over every blade of grass bends an angel whispering, Grow! Grow!" Did he think angels whisper over careers? Does he pray for his speeches or books? He said, "I'm a 'Thy will be done' person. I leave it up to someone smarter than I am. Besides, as Dossey puts it, "There is a danger of confusing God with vitamins. We dishonor prayer if we reduce it to a tool." As I thought about how a businessperson might honor prayer, it occurred to me that a prayerful reflection on one's work might provoke this question: Why should God take an interest in my career?

Answering that question might force an alignment between work and something greater. Perhaps then we could hear the whispers: "Grow! Grow!" And how shall we respond? We grow by bringing learning to helping, by achieving creative usefulness.

The Big Bang: The Theory of Expanding Usefulness

Just as individual leaders and high-achievers tend to be Warriors of Usefulness, so it is for organizations.

The "Big Bang Theory" of Business:
The history of success is the story of expanding usefulness.

Look at the great organizations, the ones that customers and employees love; they are the ones that are most helpful. Think of the companies you admire—what are they? Ritz-Carlton? eBay? Dell? Nordstrom's? Southwest Airlines? Aren't these the most helpful?

Make a list of marvelous companies and you'll see that they don't just do the same things in the same ways as everyone else—if so, why would you find them marvelous? We fall in love with what's special, not with what's ordinary. Or, as has become my motto for my own work, "Different isn't always better, but better is always different." You can't be a great organization without being different. You can't be a great anything without being different.

Take helping and innovating together and you've tapped into the "chi" of expanding usefulness. The best bosses and the best employees, the best suppliers and the best customers are attracted to innovation, to being in on the action, to the adventure of the different and better. The best managers and employees know that while different isn't always better, better is always different. Progress is a matter of willingness to experiment, which is a subset of the willingness to learn.

If you want to work among the best, you must make yourself worthy of them.

This means you and/or those in your department or organization must be one or another of the variations of Warriors: Gifted Bosses, Wild Brains or Angels of Implementation. Gifted Bosses are creative leaders, Wild Brains are experimenters at any level of an organization, and Angels of Implementation are people who are sufficiently clever to turn experiments into change. In other words, all three require innovations.

The Way of the Innovator

Let's start with a pair of instances of warrior usefulness and then analyze them to see what we can learn:

1. As a river guide, Mark Thatcher knew that those on the river had two lousy options for footwear—tennis shoes, which filled with water, making them heavy and slow to dry, or rubber thong sandals, which were liable to be washed away. So one night he decided to try to fit some straps to a pair of rubber sandals. I asked him how he went about it. He laughed, saying, "I just started poking holes." Soon he had invented the Teva Sport Sandal, and, in doing so, launched a new shoe category.

2. At age 26, Chip Conley was working for a real estate development company that wanted to build an amphitheater in Silicon Valley. Conley's assignment was to develop a strategic partnership with music promoter Bill Graham. Although the amphitheater was never built, Graham one day asked the young Conley, "What are your dreams?" Conley replied, "To build a hotel for people like me," meaning one targeted at young professionals. Graham offered a counter suggestion, a place for rock and roll bands and

other performers—travelers not welcomed in many inns. From that arose Conley's first venture, a motel called The Phoenix. Conley bought "a closed and broken-down motor lodge" on the edge of San Francisco's seedy Tenderloin district. He had a small budget, a lousy location, and a questionable facility; but he had a dream and a niche. He knew what performance venus were nearby, and, from them, who was coming to town. He had a clearly defined target market—the club managers, the travel agents, and road managers for the performers.

Once you have a target market to help, you have instant creativity. Here's Conley's explanation in his autobiography, *The Rebel Rules*: "When the then unheralded Sinead O'Connor stayed [at The Phoenix], she was losing her voice. We knew right then it was essential to have an ear, nose, and throat doctor on call for our performer-guests. The dancers who stayed with us appreciated our massage staff. The visual artists enjoyed the fact that each of our guest rooms featured the work of an emerging local artist. Band members watched our 'band-on-the-road' video collection of the world's greatest music-oriented feature films. And everyone's bus drivers appreciated our free, roomy parking lot. The complete package, including many other unique services such as free passes to underground clubs and a staff-written guide to their favorite hot spots, wasn't suited to your average traveler, but it fit the needs of this market to a tee."

The cliché "problems are opportunities" has truth in it. But most people invoke that adage as part of a stereotypical pep talk about attitudes and positive thinking. I'm suggesting something more than mere attitude—the way of creative usefulness.

Start poking holes. There's no excuse not to start experimenting. Where? The people in our examples weren't merely solving their own problems, they were solving other people's problems. You may have heard the expression that getting rich is a matter of Other People's Money. With the Warriors of Usefulness, it's a matter of Other People's Problems. This was especially vivid in our hotel example, in which Conley solved several types of problems (physical/health, entertainment, and community involvement) for several types of performers and even had something for the bus drivers.

Creativity for the Uninspired

The one obstacle that blocks almost all creativity is most people's inability to see themselves as creative, so they give up before starting. On the other hand, most people would never think of themselves as ordinary. In my experience, it's much more natural and far more productive to get people to REFUSE TO BE ORDINARY rather than to be creative, yet the result is the same.

If you can get yourself or those around you to agree to STOP BEING ORDINARY, then there is instant karma.

Creativity for the Uninspired . . .
1. Make a list of customer problems—NOT your problems; your customers' problems. (Whether these are the company's customers or your department's customers doesn't matter. Include your bosses' problems.)
2. Pick a problem to work on and recruit others to do likewise.
3. Keep a notebook of all efforts.

4. Look for chances to experiment—not change, just experiment. (People hate to change, but most love to experiment.)
5. Don't just communicate but celebrate any successes.
6. Celebrate, but take no credit.

The plan was inspired by the police department of Madison, Wisconsin. If a government agency can be creative . . . well, read on:

In Madison the police were looking for ways to improve their annual appraisal system. They came up with the problem orientation as an alternative way to think about performance. The way it works is, if you're a police officer, you take a look at your beat and try to find something you'd like to fix.

What happens if an officer says, "I can't come up with anything"? That person is told, "Go and meet with the community. Arrange meetings till you have something." Although that sounds autocratic, the process is anything but. The officers keep their notebooks, but at the end of each year, each person is asked, "Would you like this to go into your personnel file?" So an officer has a choice to truly commit to the process or just skate.

One of the captains of the Madison force, Randy Gaber, says that the number of officers who genuinely commit to the program has increased each year. That's because the successes are reported in a newsletter that goes to all employees and to the mayor and city council. But, perhaps more importantly, the program spreads because officers get to boast of their accomplishments to themselves and to everyone they know. (This may seem to conflict with "take no credit," but as you read on, notice that while the program was devised by the department's upper management, it's set up to allow individual officers to be the stars of the show. Management is both the audience and the producer/promoter.)

Gaber gave an example of an officer who got a new beat and discovered he'd inherited the traffic intersection with the highest accident rate in the city. He studied the accident reports, met with the neighbors and nearby businesses, went to Traffic Engineering and suggested an experiment. This officer had figured out that the accidents were a result of some impatient drivers cutting around the line of cars waiting to get on a major thoroughfare. So he asked for an experiment to see if he was right, and he had barrels put in place that would prevent the cutting maneuver. Sure enough, the accident rate plummeted. Traffic Engineering then put in medians and landscaping and made the change permanent.

Imagine how that officer must feel every time he passes that intersection. I suspect he takes relatives and visitors by there and points it out as he says, "That's MY intersection," and tells the story of how it went from the highest accident rate to among the lowest. Further, the department celebrated this story and others like it in its newsletter. Soon, officers were eager to find problems to solve; they were no longer just defeating criminals, they were enriching lives; they had become not just police officers, but Warriors of Usefulness.

What is extraordinary about this approach is that you don't need inspiration to begin. In fact, look at all you do NOT need to start being creatively useful:

- leadership
- management
- inspiration
- teams
- budgets

- permission
- help
- ideas

Creative without inspiration? Without ideas? Exactly. Just listen. The rest will follow. If it doesn't, here's one more approach.

Problems Hidden in Plain Sight

In some situations, customers are so accustomed to your procedures that they accept them without question. So you should also observe how they interact with you and your company. Two examples:

1. Jim Philion was head of Thrifty Car Rentals. One day he decided to sit and watch his employees rent cars. These were typical agents, standing at a typical counter, working a computer, completing forms on the monitor. As he watched with new eyes, Philion saw that customers spent most of the transaction looking at the tops of the heads of his agents. Occasionally the customer leaned forward and tried to peek at what was on the screen.

   Was there a better way? He tried an experiment. He had the counter lowered to desk height, and he had the agents introduce themselves to the customers and shake hands. They then sat together at a desk with a computer screen they both could see.

   These simple changes made a profound difference. Now the agent and customer were equals, working together on the transaction. Satisfaction increased, but to Philion's surprise, so did upgrades and insurance sales. Why? The physical layout had changed the nature of the transaction from something secretive to something mutual. A customer could see on the screen the cars available and might say, "Oh, you have convertibles? How much more is that?" And insurance sales increased because trust had. (It's a shame that Philion moved on before he got to implement the change at Thrifty. However, we get the benefit of his experiment.)

2. Anyone who travels knows what it feels like to arrive in a city in the morning, exhausted, eager to go to the hotel to cleanup and rest. But try to check in before 1 p.m. (or 2 or 3 or even 4) and you're treated as a swindler, or, at best, an interruption to the housekeeping staff's schedule. Not at the Peninsula Beverly Hills hotel, where they have a 24-hour a day check-in policy. General Manager, Ali Kasikci, was given an award by Cornell University's hotel school for this innovation. Yet, what change could be more obvious to anyone who watched customers check in?

The cost of this new policy? Nothing. The only change was in recordkeeping and the eventual replacement of the vacuum cleaners with smaller, quieter models.
All that was required was that some of the housekeeping staff came in earlier, a change some of them preferred, as it allowed them to be home earlier.

So, in addition to "just listen," let's add "just watch." Some of the greatest services to customers is to solve problems so familiar they've forgotten to complain about them.

Notice the beauty of the problems-as-solutions approach. It focuses everyone on customers, on learning and helping. In addition to asking yourself about customer problems, you can ask:

- Who are our best customers (internal and/or external)?
- Who are our worst customers?
- How could we get more good ones and fewer bad ones?
- What are we famous for?
- Where do we suck?

These are the sort of questions that turn attention outward, away from bureaucratic issues to customer ones, and turn the mind of the organization to expanding usefulness.

Such questions also turn energies away from merely studying excellence to inventing it. In most organizations, the goal is to "benchmark" the "best practices" of better organizations. But this strategy is doomed, because it is what everyone else is doing. While it feels like leadership, it is followship—instead of making you exceptional, it takes you to the highest order of ordinariness. However, when you start poking holes in the status quo, then you aren't just imitating excellence, you are participating "creative destruction," killing off the old and replacing it with something better.

The Art of Creative Usefulness is where the competitive zeal of warrior spirit joins with the joy of helping, resulting in "the smile of a conqueror," and the satisfaction of having killed the status quo.

*   *   *

From our discussion in Part One, we can now add the first four points in The Code of the Laughing Warrior.

- Think like a hero: Who can I help today?
- Work like an artist: What else can we try?
- Refuse to be ordinary: Pursue excellence, then kill it.
- Celebrate, but take no credit.

PART TWO

THE RELENTLESS DRAGONS OF MEDIOCRITY

- *Accept that organizations call to the worst in human nature, and be liberated by that knowledge*

Most organizations are founded on some notion of being different and better, but they lose momentum and turn inward, sucked back into mediocrity by bureaucracy and hierarchy, by inertia and internal resentments. This isn't simply some goof of management or screw-up by employees; it's something deeper. To understand how to create a place of warrior energy, we must first appreciate what we are up against.

If you're not beguiling by age 12, forget it.

Charles Schultz (Lucy speaking to Charlie Brown)

Consider this hypothesis: Your personality is built upon genetic hardwiring. You've heard the old advice, "You can't change anyone else"; well, you can't much change yourself either.

And if you object to that hypothesis, consider this one: One of the notions that might be hardwired into your personality is the belief that your personality is not hardwired.

I've never had much interest in wiring—hard or otherwise—until I discovered the marvelous work going on in the study of genetics and the human genome. One of my first encounters with the new field of evolutionary psychology was trying to figure out my teenaged daughter, which led me to read *The Nurture Assumption* by Judith Rich Harris. She wrote, "Study after study shows the same thing: almost all the similarities between adult siblings can be attributed to their shared genes. There are very few similarities that can be attributed to the home in which they both grew up." Then she goes on to conclude that while half of personality traits can be attributed to genetic differences between individuals, the other half can be accounted for by peer influence, making this prediction for future research: "Children would develop into the same sort of adults if we left their lives outside the home unchanged—left them in their schools and their neighborhoods—but switched all the parents around."

If our parents couldn't mold our personalities, why should we believe that the nagging of our "inner-parent" is going to change us? We nag ourselves about our personality traits that we believe we ought to control by dint of self-discipline, but many of these turn out to be genetic. For instance, this from Nigel Nicholson in the *Harvard Business Review*: "Genes for detachment and novelty avoidance have been found, which together appear to amount to shyness. It used to be assumed that shyness was induced entirely by environment—if a shy person just tried hard enough, he or she could become the life of the party. The same was said for people who were highly emotional—they could be coaxed out of such feelings. But again, research is suggesting that character traits such as shyness and emotional sensitivity are inborn."

When I did the research that led to my book *The Gifted Boss*, I found that great bosses spend little time trying to mold employees into greatness, but they instead devote extraordinary efforts to spotting and courting exceptionally capable employees. Turns out that the best management is finding employees who don't need managing. Being a parent to employees is futile and exhausting. Once you start to accept the idea that people are largely "hardwired," then you stop trying to change them and instead start to find the right use for their brain/personality "equipment."

Even so, there is a larger issue with our equipment. Our brains basically stopped evolving back in the hunter-gatherer stage. So we bring to the modern office our ancient brains. This has some highly useful implications for organizations.

Nicholson sums up in three words one battle with our programming: "Hierarchy is forever." In those cases where hierarchy is eliminated, an informal one inevitably takes its place. Then it gets even more interesting.

- Our brains are magnificent danger alert devices, which, in a modern office, amounts to a "What can go wrong?" device, giving greater weight to dangers than to opportunities.
- One of the human universals, one of the traits common to all human societies, is that we tend to learn by imitation.
- While we are naturally hierarchical, we tend to resent people at the top of the hierarchy. (In one recent British study conducted by Andrew Oswald and Daniel Zizzo, respondents who'd won money in the first phase of an experiment were given a chance to spend part of their winnings to take money from others. They didn't keep the money they took away; they spent their winnings to "burn" others' winnings. Who would be so foolish as to opt for these lose-lose propositions? Sadly, the majority of respondents. The highest use of burning was those who won small amounts of money taking from those who had been most successful. The authors referred to this as an illustration of "how much we hate winners.")

Thus, we can see the bind that is hardwired into our brains: If you put people who are naturally hierarchical and suspicious into an organization, the logical outcome is to grow a protective layer of bureaucracy. Moreover, we are programmed to learn by imitation, only to grow weary of being imitators. We eventually learn not to learn, becoming masters of the same old solution, becoming conformists. In short, we are genetically predisposed to create environments of which we want no part. Or, put more simply, it's natural that organizations suck.

Depressing and discouraging? No. There is something liberating about realizing that organizations naturally move to the awful. It means that you can stop berating yourself or those around you for being hierarchical or bureaucratic or resistant to change or resentful—hey, it's just human nature.

Allow me to digress for a moment to tell you how I learned just how effective it can be to accept human nature.

I had an hour to kill one evening and so I indulged one of my joys—going to a good bookstore. Friends had pressed me to read two books, and I stopped at the information desk to inquire about them. The harried young clerk told me, "We have both. *The Red Queen* is in Science and *The Power of Now* is in Self-Help." She offered to take me to each section, but I said I'd go it alone. So she pointed out Science, just to her left, and Self-Help, in the opposite corner.

I quickly found *The Red Queen* and noticed that the author, Matt Ridley, had another book called *Genome*. I started to take both, but then forced myself to return *Genome* to the shelf—after all, I had dozens of books on genetics and plenty of books waiting to be read. Then I walked across the store to find the other book. The books in Self-Help were alphabetical by author and I worked along to the spot where *The Power of Now* should be. Not there. Instead, in the very slot where it should have been was *Genome*.

I concluded from this that I needed to read the book and voila, there was the explanation as to why "organizations suck" should be useful and encouraging information. The author of *Genome* reported on work by Efran, Greene, and Gordon from a publication for psychologists and counselors (*The Psychotherapy Networker*). One of the authors, Jay Efran, noted that he had always been shy and as a boy he had been pushed to be more outgoing, to speak up, and generally given all the try-harder advice parents give shy kids. As an adult, still shy, he led "assertiveness training and social-skills interaction" groups, which included coaching in "asking for dates, initiating phone calls, sending back overcooked steaks and so on." The results were "disappointing" with "few real breakthroughs."

Then, having discovered the research on the genetic underpinning of shyness, Efran and his colleagues decided on a new approach. Basically, the counselors told their assertiveness training clients that they were naturally shy; that it was genetic and there was nothing they could do about it.

The results among the group that got the truth about their genes were extraordinary: "Paradoxically, giving group members permission to be the way they are seemed to constitute the best insurance that their self-esteem and interpersonal effectiveness would improve." What happened was that shy people stopped trying to be faux-extroverts and started compensating. Instead of focusing on themselves, they started seeing how their shy behavior was misinterpreted as arrogance or coldness. Instead of pretending to be outgoing and hating themselves for their weakness, they confessed their shyness, and this led to genuine interaction.

Something similar happens when you accept that it's natural for organizations to suck. You can stop blaming yourself or those around you, stop trying to change personalities, and start creating environments that draw people away from the worst and toward the best of human nature. I asked Efran how acceptance of hardwiring changes how people view the people around them. He said, "If you realize that a lot of who we are is genetic, then you can arrange a good fit between yourself and your environments." He added that, "The most important change may be that you can become lighter about being victimized by your inner-voice about who you are. You accept that it's 'A big SO WHAT?'"

Applying this to organizational life, once you accept that organizational people are hardwired for mediocrity and conformity, then you can look at the role of leadership differently. The popular management advice, "Hire good people and get out of their way" is flawed. Without meaning to, most employees, even good ones, opt for the safety of mediocrity. So the real wisdom is "Hire good people and keep re-showing them the way." (Never forget that "the way" is the best of themselves.)

* * *

With the fifth principle of the Code, and with the accompanying revelations in hand, we can turn our attention to distracting our ancient brains from their programming.

- Accept that organizations call to the worst in human nature, and be liberated by that knowledge.

PART THREE
MANAGING "CHI"—COAXING OUT THE
WARRIOR SPIRIT AROUND YOU

- *Looking Through Eyes that Encourage, Spot the
  Gifts of Others and Hold them Up for All to Admire*
- *Practice Gandhi Curiosity—Experiments Never Fail*

Knowing that the worst of human nature—the dragons of mediocrity, complacency, and bureaucracy—are going to come looking for you, there is but one sure defense: helping and usefulness, learning and laughter—the best of human nature.

Management by Asking Questions

A computer consultant named Arno Rite was speaking reverently of one of his past bosses. What made this boss so special? "He was always learning. He made you think because he always wanted to learn." That is a distinguishing trait of leaders: they are learners. It may seem odd that the student is the teacher, but the fact is that the one who asks the questions leads the conversation.

If you want to fail, come across as a "know-it-all"—you will inspire those around you to prove you wrong. Instead, strive to be the opposite—not a "know-nothing," but a "learn-it-all"—and those around you will rise to help you.

When you talk to gifted bosses, one of the morals of their stories often comes down to "Ask, don't tell." John Hawke, who was CEO of Howe Barnes, a Chicago brokerage company, described his first management job at one of the major brokerages and how he botched his first task, which was to transfer an assistant from one pair of brokers to another. He went to the pair of brokers and in classic "I'm the boss" fashion, declared what he had decided to do. The senior of the two brokers, one of the firm's stars, gave the neophyte boss a short and heated lecture on being presumptuous, then huffed out. The remaining broker watched his associate leave, then turned back to Hawke and said with disgust, "I can't believe you'd treat a person of such quality with such disrespect." And he too walked out.

So, within hours of becoming a manager, Hawke had alienated two key employees. Trying to figure out what had gone wrong, he sought his mentor's advice, who explained, "Whenever there's any change, start by asking, 'What would you think if . . .?'"

This seems simple, but it represents a philosophy that eludes most bosses, one Hawke now summarizes as, "We succeed together." Or, in the words of another gifted boss, Bob Klas, CEO of TapeMark, "People will exercise great effort and creativity to make OUR plan work; and sometimes expend just as much effort and creativity to make YOUR plan fail."

In discussing motivation, Hawke also said, "When you want people to move to the next level of performance, go to them with a notebook in hand. Get them to step outside themselves. Ask, 'If this were a movie, what would happen next in your career?'"

Whenever there's to be change, GO WITH A NOTEBOOK IN HAND. If you go with empty hands, it means that you don't intend to hear anything worth saving, that you've gone into that meeting to make pronouncements rather than to work together to the best possible outcome. Empty hands; closed mind.

Shashi Gupta applies a Zen-like wisdom to running Apex Data Services, a data conversion services company. He calls his business a "social experiment," and it is his goal to have the employees "responsible to the work, not to management." And so employees set their own hours, choose their own vacations and to some extent even their own salaries. About the only rule in the company is this one: "If you want to implement an idea, you must be able to answer three questions."

What are the three questions?

The answer: NO ONE KNOWS, including Gupta!

Isn't that marvelous? You see the brilliance of this approach. You unburden your-self by being the one asking the questions instead of the one answering them. It's what your employees want; they just don't know it yet.

By the way, unlike Gupta, I want employees and suppliers to anticipate one ques-tion: WHAT ELSE COULD WE TRY? I want them to come to any meeting with multiple solutions.

At first, they will object, asking, "What's wrong with my plan?"

Nothing is wrong. What else could we try?

Asking The Impossible

Ginger Graham, until recently one of the Group Chairmen of Guidant Corporation, understands organizational energy. For one, she knows that companies run not on rules but on stories: "They are like cave paintings on the wall—great sto-ries make great companies." Her favorite is the time that the company introduced a breakthrough product for heart patients, one that Marketing expected to capture three-quarters of the market. What no one anticipated was that the product was so good that the market itself would grow 25 percent overnight. The company received so many orders that management knew they would run out of product. In Graham's words, "No matter how we did the math, how many shifts we ran, the answer was the same: NO WAY!"

So, instead of calculations, Graham called the employees together and explained the problem in human terms and then asked for help. The employees responded with ideas, then set about to turn out more product than was possible.

Management jumped in with double- and triple-time pay, with meals served at the plants, car service to pick up kids, and even, given that this was the holiday season, a gift-wrapping service in the plant. Graham recalled taking her turn working at the gift-wrap shop, chuckling at the recollection of some of the gifts to be wrapped—a surfboard, for instance—but concluded that the season of exceptional effort was "the most fun we've ever had."

The facts were clear: meeting demand was impossible. To expect more was irrational. But the truth is more than mere facts; the possibilities are more than the merely rational. And the result is more than output; it's "the most fun we've ever had."

Questions in Action: Experiments

Experiments never fail. It isn't that everything you try will work out exactly the way you planned . . . of course not. But when you experiment, you give yourself the opportunity to be surprised, like scratching off a lottery ticket. And you also short-circuit the resistance to change, both from those above and below.

Don Urbanciz is an example of one Laughing Warrior who used experiments to combat bureaucracy:

He was assigned to head the Chicago operations of a major insurance company. He came in, looked around, and decided that his new organization was so rigid that it restricted the flow of ideas. So Urbanciz said to the staff, "What would happen if we went without an organization chart? Let's try it and see what happens."

There's genius in "Let's see what happens." Imagine if he'd said, "I'm tearing up the organization chart—here's what we're doing instead." The staff would have expected him to have all the answers. But, as an experiment, he didn't need to know where the idea would take them; he was open to surprise. And get this: he set himself up to be a hero. If going without the organization chart helped set a new tone of openness, then he's a hero. If it's a disaster, and he then goes to the staff and says, "This isn't working—we need to reinvent the organization chart," then he's a hero for listening and learning. Maybe he expected the latter result and simply wanted the new org-chart to be welcomed—we don't know. We just know that his experiment couldn't fail.

On another occasion Urbanciz found himself in the midst of a corporate territorial dispute, the sort in which employees count the ceiling tiles in their offices. So he decided to conduct an experiment whereby he offered any employee who'd give up a window office a $2,000 increase in pay, to be offset by employees willing to take a $2,000 cut in pay to move into a window office. Every person in a window office volunteered to move out; no one volunteered to move in. The offices that had seemed so valuable had been given a monetary worth, and it was something well below $2,000 a year. End of obsession with ceiling tiles.

Gandhi Curiosity

Notice how this experimenter's mindset fits with the curiosity and openness that is necessary not just for Gifted Bosses but for Wild Brains and Angels of Implementation as well.

An experiment is non-passive learning; it's Gandhi curiosity. A plan is an edict; an experiment is an adventure. Even if what you attempt is a disaster, at least you have a new appreciation for what you were doing before you may have a story to tell but, most of all, you have practiced your escape from routine, practiced your ability to be different, traveled to the new.

Experimenting With Dreams

Perhaps you work in an organization buffeted by upheavals, one where your cheese has been moved so many times that people say, "Change is good" with a smirk. Such people haven't gotten skilled at change but at pretending to be good at it.

I believe that most of us come into the workplace with the desire to make a difference, to do something exceptional, to be special. And what do organizations do with that flame? They beat it out of existence. They say they encourage people to develop their talents, but then they stamp them into the mold labeled "team player," meaning somebody who does what he or she is told without being told.

However, occasionally a leader comes along who calls to the best in us, who relights the torch. Perhaps you are called to be one, to be a guardian of the flame. I know it sounds grand and poetic, but it is, nonetheless, quite practical. You can redirect energy in a matter of hours. Try this experiment.

In the press of everyday work, we literally forget to dream. One gifted boss, John Genzale, editor of a thriving trade magazine, *SportsBusiness*, called together his staff and had them go around the room and describe a project they'd love to work on— that one big story that they haven't had the time or resources or expertise to undertake. He explained that he wanted them to "dream up a project that you want to tell your mother about, a piece that you will look back on with pride in ten years."

Why do it in a group setting? Genzale says, "Everyone wants to help. They add ideas, make suggestions, offer help. They root for the person to pull it off. There is a magic that goes on." I've seen that magic many times. It's the excellence virus. You listen to a person's dream, feel the energy, and you want to help, and you also want to know that feeling for yourself.

By the way, I should point out that the first time Genzale asked every employee for a dream, only a few actually carried it out. The second time it was a few more. That's OK. Not all the kernels have to pop at the same time in order to end up with a bowl of popcorn.

Refuse to be Ordinary

Another way to reawaken the dormant warrior mind is to call to the natural urge to STOP BEING ORDINARY and START BEING USEFUL. No one wants to be told what to do, especially to be told to work longer or harder, but most everyone wants to help and to learn.

Here are two case studies of leaders who made a conscious decision not to be followers.

Charlie Eitel became CEO of Simmons Company (Beautyrest mattresses and the like) after taking a flooring company called Interface from 635 million to 1.3 billion in revenues over his six years as CEO. What's relevant here is that when he arrived at Interface he discovered that the company had evolved into being a follower—it would manufacture "me too" versions of successful styles. One of his first major decisions was to declare to all employees that they "would never again attempt to imitate any competitor's products."

He says, "If you create a culture when it's OK to knock off competitor's products, that mindset flows right to the emotion of employees. Nobody likes to work for a copycat—GREAT COMPANIES DON'T FOLLOW."

Some pinheads might think it laughable that a CEO would be discussing emotions flowing from a product like carpeting, instead assuming that employee morale is a condition of wages or benefits or working conditions. But if you have a choice—and remember, great employees always have a choice—why would you work on second-rate products? No matter what the industry, if you aren't working on projects that will land you on the cover of your trade magazine, then you don't deserve the best employees.

And the way to the cover of the trade press is STOP BEING ORDINARY. And it's the way to the hearts of consumers too—give them something to love. Much of what you sell are "me too" products. Where do these score on the Usefulness Meter? Barely a blip, until you find a way to make them easier or cheaper or faster or something that will change them from "me too" to "look at me" products.

The other example is the Aeron office chair made by Herman Miller—you know the one that's made of mesh, with the back that's like an upside-down guitar. How did Bill Stumpf and Don Chadwick come up with so magnificent a design? First, the will to difference came when they visited a company in Denver that was about to purchase ergonomic chairs and had assembled sixty models in one room. In a glance they realized that all sixty looked basically alike. It was then that the two designers declared that their chair, if placed in that room, would stand-alone.

And then the men set about playing with designs. They had learned from a study of truck drivers that fidgeting was a matter not only of pressure but heat. So they knew they wanted air circulation. They turned to patio furniture for ideas, then created scale models, using material cut from panty hose to represent the breathing material they sought. And it was feeling those little scale models, how the panty hose material conformed to the touch, that they found their aspiration.

It took an engineer more than 40 variations to create a workable material, but, once done, the designers fit the new material to a distinctive shape, and they had a chair that struck me, on first sight, as ugly. But it was so ugly I had to sit in it, and, well, it was love at first sit. And there's a lesson about ugliness: when design raises standards, it often raises doubts, and only later do you realize that you've encountered a new beauty, waiting for you to catch up.

And catch up with this thought: the beauty grew out of helpfulness.

You pursue excellence, then kill it by doing something better.

Keep asking,
WHO CAN WE HELP?
and
WHAT ELSE CAN WE TRY?
and in evaluating the answers,
KEEP REFUSING TO BE ORDINARY.

If you are trying different ways to help, but you are merely fitting old solutions to old problems, you don't get a circle of helping, you get clichés. Remember that real achievement requires the EXPANDING usefulness of experimentation.

What Makes People Want to Give Their Best?

In his marvelous book, *Climbing the Blue Mountain*, Eknath Easwaran writes about his teaching at University of California at Berkeley:

One of the most rewarding parts of my job as a professor was to go to debating competitions and sit right up front, with a few sympathetic colleagues by my side. Up comes Kamala, my favorite student, not used to public speaking but capable of a good performance given the right occasion. The boys in front are wearing expectant smiles: "Imagine Kamala representing our school!" Kamala reads their look and thinks perhaps she had better go back and sit down. Then she catches my eye. My look says, "Come on, Kamala. You know I like your stories. They will too." This is all it takes: somebody whose eyes encourage, whose attitude is eager and unreserved.

Think about how much business leaders could accomplish by having "eyes that encourage." If you are an admired leader and you tell employees, "You can do this," they will believe you. An admired executive is like a king who can touch commoners on the shoulders with a sword and declare them knights. But how many do? How many are "eager and unreserved"?

The Art of the Compliment

It was the late Tim Gullickson who transformed Pete Sampras into a great tennis player. When asked in an ESPN interview how Gullickson altered his game, Sampras replied, "He talked about my strengths. He reminded me how good I was."

It's easy to picture Sampras's previous coaches pointing out his weaknesses, thinking that criticism was constructive. That's the way most coaching works, and most management, too. What you often "construct" with criticism is self-doubt and/or resentment, resulting, at best, in excellent mediocrity. On the other end of the continuum is management by strengths. It's easy to forget just how good we can be. After all, we are rarely asked for our best work, just for our fastest or cheapest.

If you write a report, and someone says, "good job" or "great report", that's nice, but nothing compared to "I liked your report so much that I passed it on to the president," or, "I'd like to have a meeting with all the salespeople and have you talk about how you work." Such praise doesn't make a person conceited; it makes a person better.

I've been collecting compliments. Here are a few of the stories I've heard so far.

- The most elaborate example comes from Marie McNeil, whose bosses were so grateful for her work that one week they gave her a gift every day, and on Friday they gave her the afternoon off to go shopping with the mall gift certificates that were the final gift. She said, "I know [my bosses] sound too good to be true, but sometimes I wish they weren't. I started working for them while I was going to school for computer programming with the understanding that I would find a job in the computer industry after I graduated. Well, I graduated, but I'm having a hard time moving on."

- Barry Krischer, when he was State Attorney of Palm Beach County in Florida, sent out thank you letters to a group of attorneys and investigators who helped him with a round-up of parole violators. But what made it unique was that he included a "certificate" good for a half-day off work. These people didn't work for him, so the certificate was a gag, but you can bet that those people left that joke out for everyone to see.

- Rhonda Spencer once had her CEO introduce her to someone saying, "This is one of the sharpest people you'll ever meet." She added, "Imagine how hard I work every day to live up to that."

- Alexis Driscoll wrote, "A colleague introduced me as 'someone who can think through walls.' I smile even as I type this."

- And the simplest, but perhaps most powerful, came from Jim Masmar, who was told, "We need your personal touch for this project." How could you hear that and NOT make the project special?

The maxim of *The One-Minute Manager*, "Catch somebody doing something right," is a great and timeless principle of leadership and perhaps The Art of the Compliment is just reinventing it. But we could be on to something even more profound. Let's call it, *Catch a glimpse of someone's character and hold it up for him or her to admire.*

Beverly Chiodo, a professor of communications at Southwest Texas State, requires her students to name and write about a hero in their lives. The effect is that the class ends up thinking about and discussing what it takes to be admirable, a question that just isn't asked in our society. "What does it take to get rich?" is asked. Popular? Sexy? Successful? Yes. Admirable? No. Chiodo put it this way: "Character is the foundation to accomplishment."

One student described this character-elevating moment: "I had an instructor who told me, 'Paul, you're an honest man.' Ever since then, I find that I am incapable of being dishonest.'" That's the power of praising character—it gets in amongst a person's self-image and self-worth. It becomes you, in both meanings of that expression.

But what about "you can't change people?" This isn't about trying to make people be something they aren't; it's about picking out an admirable trait and getting them to dwell on it. It's taking your strength of character and giving it away. That's something more than management, more than catching people doing something right; that's creating a place fit for heroes by issuing a call to The Warrior Spirit.

Barbara Torres, an executive with TRW, loves to get people excited about their work by "getting them to see something in themselves they haven't seen before." One of her former bosses had done just that with her, although in a sly way. One day in a meeting, her boss, Charlie Graves, a retired army general, spoke to the group about her, using her to illustrate a point: "Take Barbara: She's great at managing technical capabilities; it's just a shame that she doesn't have the ability to build business." This sounds like something of an insult, like he was "catching someone doing something WRONG," but he was really speaking to her defiant streak. If he had asked her to work on her skills at business development/marketing, she would have rebelled. However, by dropping that comment, he set her upon a personal campaign to develop that skill and to prove him wrong. She began by studying those in the company who were great at business development and began experimenting with their techniques. She soon had techniques of her own, and she put herself "in an environment where I needed to use those skills."

When had her boss let her in on his little manipulation? He was working her; however, when she had once insisted that he had known he was working her, he just smiled and winked. He could have tried to teach her, but instead, he figured out how to get her to learn.

I wonder if, on the way to that meeting, the old general didn't turn Laughing Warrior and ask himself, "Who can I help today?" I can picture his eyes lighting up at the answer: "Oh, I could tweak Barbara Torres! Maybe I could get her mad enough to see just how great she could be!"

Set Up To Be A Hero

Picture this: It's a company-wide managers' meeting and the guy in charge of Management Information is up front. After 20 minutes of complaints and suggestions from a hundred people, one of the managers stands up and says, "We've been complaining, but I want you to know that we appreciate all you've done for us." The group starts applauding and then rises for a spontaneous standing ovation.

When was the last time you saw anyone get a standing ovation in a routine meeting—not after a speech or at an awards ceremony, but in a managers' update? How about the last time you saw an information manager get a standing ovation? This one didn't just happen; it was four years in the making.

Before I tell you about those four years and about Dan Fesler, who believes in setting people up to be heroes, let's consider how things work at most companies. In their book *The Set-Up-To-Fail Syndrome*, Manzoni and Barsoux write, "The set-up-to-fail syndrome begins innocuously enough. The triggering event could be specific—perhaps an employee misses a target or a deadline, loses a client, or gives a poor report or presentation. The trigger could also be quite vague—maybe the employee arrived from another unit with a lukewarm recommendation or reacted oddly to early advice from the boss. In any case, something sows a doubt in the boss's mind."

At which point bosses do what bosses do; they manage more, meaning doing more supervising, checking-up and offering advice. The result could be an upward spiral of improving performance, but it's often a slide into self-doubt and resentment. At which point, how do the managers respond? With more managing, of course. And why not? Who would react to declining performance by saying, "This person obviously needs less supervision"? Further, as the authors point out, there is a "confirmatory bias," which is another way of saying that we tend to see what we expect to see. Here, management sees mistakes and the need for supervision and thus the spiral into job failure is accelerated.

Now we can compare the "set-up-to-fail syndrome" with Dan Fesler's "set-up-to-be-a-hero syndrome." Fesler, who runs Lampert Yards, a chain of lumber stores in the upper Midwest, sat down with his new employee and said, "Half the people here hate your department. Can we set it up so everybody likes you? If so, you'll accomplish twice as much."

Together they came up with a plan. First, they had a meeting with all the managers to create an information Wish List. Then they went back to the group and said, "We have 101 'Number One Priorities.' We'd need a staff of at least eighteen employees to accomplish them all, and we have a staff of four. So we need to agree on the ten most critical goals." They thus turned a Wish List into practical but ambitious goals. Now at each staff meeting, the managers get a brief report on progress, and they get to see items being checked off the list.

The result has been to turn the group's focus from what HAS NOT been done to what HAS. As Fesler put it, "I was bringing an employee into an ugly situation and I wanted to find a way to turn it into an opportunity to be a hero."

It was four years from the day the new manager took over to the day of the standing ovation. The moment of applause was four years in the making, starting in that moment when Fesler said, "Can we set it up so everyone likes you?" This is Management by Asking Questions at its best. Fesler was aware of the negative emotional energy around the job. He asked his employee for help. Together they came up with a plan. They created a forum to talk about strengths instead of weaknesses, a showcase for the new employee's gifts. And while I wasn't there to see his expression, I am certain that when Dan Fesler asked his new employee about "accomplishing twice as much," he was looking with "eyes that encourage."

*   *   *

Two principles for the Code to add to our list:

- Looking with eyes that encourage, spot the gifts of others and hold them up for all to admire.

- Practice Gandhi curiosity—experiments never fail.

PART FOUR
WORTHY ALLIES

- *Be the one who is most THERE*
- *Seek worthy allies and seek to be worthy of them*

The Art of Spotting and Courting Worthy Allies

When James Evans was CEO of Best Western Hotels, his niece undertook her first professional job, and he wanted to sum up for her his advice about work. He got it down to these two sentences: "You don't have to be the one who works the most hours, just the one who is most there during the hours you work. Come to work and put your heart on the table."

Most THERE. Ask great bosses to describe their best employees and they describe people who are engaged and alive, fully there, eager to help and learn. They describe Warriors of Usefulness. Further, when detailing specific accomplishments, they describe Wild Brains or Angels of Implementation. Where do you find such organizational heroes? You won't find Laughing Warriors, Wild Brains, or Angels in the classified ads.

First, it is wise to assume that the unemployment rate among the top one percent of talent is always hovering just above zero. Such stars rarely walk in and ask for a job; they have to be spotted and courted.

The best bosses don't complain about the job market or the economy, not when it comes to hiring—the search for the one-in-a-hundred employee hasn't changed. Some talent scouts have it relatively easy, for instance in retail. Some managers even carry "recruitment cards," little promo pieces about what a great place they have, and a phone number to call. Perhaps you don't have quite so easy a time spotting talent. But if you're part of a large organization, you have other divisions to hire from, plus your suppliers. Everyone you meet is a potential star employee. Dennis Dougherty of Visual Electronics was working his company's booth at a trade show and could overhear the sales rep in the next booth, selling copiers. He realized this other guy was far superior to him at selling, started up a conversation, and ultimately hired him to be head of sales.

Ofer Ben-Shachar, who heads a company called Noosh, says his hiring goal is, "To hire superstars—I want to kiss the ground they walk on." To this end, he employs two in-house recruiters and devotes about 20 percent of his own time to hiring. But what most struck me about Ben-Shachar was how he came to hire a leading executive from the printing industry. He was hiring sales people—the number two and three people in his sales force—and personally called the references of his top candidates. When he had those people on the phone, he asked each one, "Who is the best executive in the printing industry?" And that's how he chose his target for the head of his sales department, who he has since recruited for Noosh.

The best bosses spend a lot of time scouting and courting, but they have the time; after all, the best employees don't need managing, at least not the old time-consuming bureaucratic kind of managing.

Here is the most important advice on hiring: See the work, not just the person. SEE THE WORK with your own eyes, or at least talk to those who have seen it, which is to see it through the eyes of others. SEE THE WORK. SEE THE WORK.

The Dangers of Interviewing

Let me back up for a moment and contrast "see the work" to the common way of hiring, which is "see the résumé." If you get résumés that have been sitting in a file, you may be interviewing everyone else's leftovers. The common procedure is to hire the best of the pool of résumé candidates, without giving much thought to the pool. To combat this, judge applicants not against the pool, but against the best employee you've ever had. You aren't looking for candidates for a job but candidates for Best Ever Employee.

This brings us to a difficult concept. If you'll keep in mind our discussion of how your brain's programming thwarts much of what you do, you can face up to this: Judge not, because you aren't very good at it.

The best people match no stereotype because being exceptional is the opposite of being stereotypical. Scheig Associates helps companies hire star performers. They identify current stars in a given job, ask them what makes for their success, and then converts the answers into pre-employment testing and interview guidelines. In other words, the hiring is based on successful behaviors, not personalities. One of the executives for Scheig described his work with groups of star performers by saying, "The first thing you realize is that personality is NOT related to output." For instance, one of their studies was with salespeople for car dealers. One of the researchers described his own surprise watching the focus groups of top salespeople: "Of the ten star performers, only one was the sort you'd call a 'salesman type.' One of the others was a woman so soft-spoken you had to lean in to hear what she was saying." Which confirms that the best salespeople are the ones who don't seem like salespeople. BUT, just when you think you have the secret—hire against type—

you remember that one guy who is a stereotype AND a star.

Second, there's research that shows attractive people are more likely to be hired for managerial positions and elected to public office, even though interviewers and voters deny that appearance is a factor. One study (by Hammermesh and Biddle) even quantified the advantage: Highly attractive people are paid 12 percent more than unattractive people. (This leads to an intriguing principle of hiring: Ugly people are a bargain.)

The point is that we can't trust appearances, and moreover, we can't trust our guts either. No wonder the best bosses have come to mistrust the traditional hiring process. Instead of sorting résumés, they spot and court talent, often taking years to reel in a great employee. This fits Scheig's review of research that evaluates the various hiring criteria most employers use. The impressions formed by the hiring managers during job interviews came out with validity scores only slightly above random. In other words, you could do about as well in your hiring decisions if you never met the candidate.

While this seems counterintuitive, it fits with all those examples of dart boards beating stock analysts, and it also fits with some research I encountered early in my career. I was doing a project on "credit worthiness"—trying to predict which people will or won't repay a loan. In one study, the absolute WORST predictor of repayment was the loan officers' judgment.

The only conclusion is that we are unable to read people. This doesn't sit well—everyone is convinced he or she is a skilled judge of character. But what is the face of character? You might as well ask, What is the shape of water?

So whenever you start your hiring, remember this: The person you interview is never the person you hire.

The point here is NOT simply that people lie on résumés or that people learn how to conceal weaknesses in interviews. (Although it's useful to remember that the job market is the used car lot of employment.) No, we're not talking about BS-ers, at least not in the sense of someone deliberately lying to you. It's dealing with self-deceived employees and suppliers that will be one of your most common difficulties in trying to get people to accomplish their goals. Installing a lie detector in your office would make you a worse manager, not better. The greater danger comes not from those who seek to lie to you, but from those who have lied to themselves.

For instance, you will have someone tell you that he really, truly wants to be in sales, and that the one thing he would love to do is to make sales calls. And so you give the guy a chance. Months go by and no sales result. So you set goals, get promises, and still…nothing. And eventually you realize, after months of effort, that he doesn't really want to sell, he wants to be a successful sales rep. He didn't lie to you; he lied to himself. He would have passed a lie detector test, so how were you to know?

Then, on top of never knowing if the person across the table really knows himself, you can't be sure about your own self-deception. We needn't resort to any swoopy genetic theorizing; we all know how easy it is to see what we want to see. Here, from Steven Pinker's *How the Mind Works*, is a tidy summary of how one of our most famous scientists, who made a career of observing, still saw what she wanted to see:

> In anthropology, one South Sea island paradise after another has turned out to be nasty and brutish. Margaret Mead said that nonchalant sex made the Samoans satisfied and free of crime; it turned out that the boys tutored one another in rape techniques. She called the Arapesh "gentle"; they were head-

hunters. She said that the Tshambuli reversed our sex roles, the men wearing curls and makeup. In fact the men beat their wives, exterminated neighboring tribes, and treated homicide as a milestone in a young man's life, which entitled him to wear the face paint that Mead thought was so effeminate.

The work, not the person. See the work.

A Place Fit for Heroes

What do great employees want? Well, money, of course. But remember this: If the people you'd love to hire were the sort to leap at a 10 percent increase in pay, they wouldn't be people you'd love to hire.

It is NOT that great employees are indifferent to money. It's not even that they get paid about the same as their second-rate similars: it's that they have lots of opportunities to be well paid, so they make their decisions on something else.

You can't offer big talent a little bribe; you have to offer either a big bribe or a big chance. The best employees know they will be well compensated, so the key decision criteria go beyond money. Even if you can't offer employees the chance to get rich, you can offer to enrich their lives. This can be the chance to contribute more, or to work in a place of energy and helping and joy, or it can also be more tangible—flexible hours, telecommuting and so on. (You'd be amazed how many great employees will change jobs for a chance to be there when their children come home from school, or to be able to take time off for Little League games, or to work on writing a novel, or have time to travel or to compete in bicycle races.) Hiring is circular helping—the goal is to find the person who will contribute the most AND benefit the most.

As for contributing, we tend to think of leadership as the old command-and-control, military model—General Patton driving the frightened troops to extraordinary achievements. But the reality is that the troops have to make the decision; they have to agree to drive themselves. Here is the wisdom of the best bosses: Organizations thrive when employees choose to bestow the gift of excellence upon them.

Take the example of Heinz Brungs, CEO of the company that makes Ironite fertilizer. Brungs tells of the time a major customer requested Ironite in boxes instead of bags. That's when he discovered that boxing machines cost close to a million dollars. Sharing this dilemma with his plant manager, Hans Schmacher, a former engineer, they discussed how to locate a used machine. Then, two weeks later, the plant manager came in to say, "I can build us a machine." And for less than one-quarter the cost of a new machine, he built one that Brungs insists is "better than any you can buy on the market."

"Is Hans proud?" Brungs asks. "You bet. The only one prouder is me." And he adds, "You get this only if you involve and respect employees. You can't order them to build a machine. You can't insist that they be creative and enthusiastic; you can only let them be creative and enthusiastic."

While many executives can tell you at what percent of capacity their plants are operating, none can tell you the percent of capacity at which their employees' brains operate; after all, creativity and initiative are unlimited resources. And that's why Heinz Brungs loves to hear this sentence: "Come out here and I'll show you what I did." To a true leader, there are no sweeter words to hear than "follow me."

Of course, Brungs runs the company so who gets credit is irrelevant to him. But what if Ironite were just one department or one division of a big corporation —what would change? Brungs succeeds because he has built an environment fit for heroes.

*   *   *

You think you don't have anything more to learn in this game, and along comes Larry Bird [as your coach]. The game preparation, the little things. Maybe you're up a little bit, in the mid-

dle of a run, and you're coming down and—boom—you pull up and take that three to break their back. Larry did it. He wanted me to do it. And you know what? If you miss, he doesn't care. If you're going to be a hero, you've got to take hero shots.

— Reggie Miller, NBA player

* * *

Ask some of your friends, when was the last time someone encouraged you to take a hero shot? Most of us are urged to do just the opposite—to think small. Without intending to, most management is anti-hero. There's plenty of credit to be gotten by understanding that sometimes you have to let an employee have a shot at being a hero. If you create a place fit for heroes, you are one.

Recruiting: Secrets of the Masters

Speaking of recruiting, I'm not keen on trying to draw analogies to business from athletics; however, we can learn plenty about courting talent from coaches. I've gotten to speak with several great ones, and their experiences are highly relevant because the college coaches can't outbid other schools for a player's services, they have to out-lure the others. If you find yourself in the luring business, you could learn from them.

LOU HOLTZ. When I interviewed legendary football coach Lou Holtz (formerly of Notre Dame, now at South Carolina), and asked him how he recruits players, he told me of sitting in the living room of Jerome "The Bus" Bettis, discussing the discipline it takes to be a better student, athlete, and person. I remarked, "I can't imagine persuading an eighteen-year old by selling discipline." He laughed his infectious laugh and said, "The mothers love it." But then he turned serious, making a remark that left me feeling small: "The best people understand that you can't be successful without sacrifice. The best never complain about sacrifices—they're proud of them."

LUTE OLSON. The University of Arizona basketball team has the best record in major college basketball over the decade of the nineties, including three trips to the Final Four and a National Championship. Lute Olson has managed to get a stream of great players to come to Tucson, which is a delightful city, but not the epicenter of the sports world. How does he get these kids who want to play in the NBA to come to a city without an NBA team?

Naturally, he sells them on great weather during the school year. But more than the location itself, he sells them on the fans, on having a facility that has been sold out for 15 straight years. So he can tell a recruit, "You will never play at home in front of an empty seat." But ask Olson about specific players, and you begin to see what he is too modest to say; the players come because of him, and specifically, how he treats the players.

Olson's dignity and control put him in contrast to the typical coach. Olson's players come to Arizona because they watch games on television and pay attention to how the coaches treat the players. The result is that Olson gets recruits who come with self-discipline and motivation, and who respond to a positive environment. He also gets players he describes as "sensitive," which would not seem to be a desirable trait in basketball, but Olson insists that this makes them more open, more willing to learn, and more passionate about the game.

JOHN WOODEN. The greatest coach ever, John Wooden (UCLA basketball, ten national championships), took me into the den of his condominium in Encino, which his late wife had turned into a trophy room. When I saw she had framed several invitations to the White House, I asked Wooden how it had been.

"Never went," he replied, then added, "When we won the championships they invited the whole team, but it would have taken two or three days and I figured the players had already missed enough school during the tournament."

I confess that I would have been on that plane to D.C. in a minute, but that story epitomizes what made him what he is: he truly had priorities. And that's why players came to him. He devoted almost no time to recruiting—he never visited prospects, refused to even contact any player outside California, no exceptions. Players had to contact him, through coaches or principals or counselors. (Lew Alcindor's coach called to say that Lew—later, Kareem, of course—would visit five colleges and then make up his mind. Wooden said only, "Could I ask a favor—that UCLA be the last of the five." That was aggressive recruiting for Wooden.)

Most of his players he met at summer camps, where the young men and their parents got to know him, and to understand that coming to play for Wooden meant they could get, as he put it, "more than just basketball." *More than just basketball.*

While many corporate managers now think of themselves as coaches, the best coaches have always thought of themselves as teachers. Perhaps it would be wise to eliminate the intermediate step; after all, the most accomplished entrepreneurs, executives, and salespeople are the most effective educators.

* * *

What inspiration can we take from these three master coaches about recruiting great talent? They have built programs around enriching rather than defeating. In fact, John Wooden says he never spoke to his team about winning or losing, but he always spoke of learning and improving. And Lute Olson explained that he had never wanted to coach college basketball, just teach and coach in a high school. I reacted by saying, "So you weren't especially ambitious?" He laughed at the idea, saying, "Oh, I was VERY ambitious: I wanted to build a great high school program. To do that, I figured I had to improve each year, to be a better coach this year than last." After 13 years of improving as a high school coach, Olson decided he wanted to move to a junior college. He eventually moved on to a small college, then Iowa, then Arizona. Is he still improving? "At the end of every season I sit down with the assistant coaches and we try to figure out what we could do better. We research other programs to see which are outstanding in each part of the game. This year we realized that Michigan State was doing a great job with rebounding. So we sent one of the coaches up there to learn how we could improve." This is the endless curiosity of creative usefulness. The best players feel it and want to be a part of it.

So, while other companies are talking about salary and benefits packages, and maybe that they have a concierge or a dog-walking service, here's what I hope you'll be able to say to your recruits, inserting examples from the experiments and heroism you are starting to see:

You are going to get the chance to accomplish more than you ever have before—NOT by working more hours, but by functioning at a superior level, fully alive, surrounded by other talented people who've been freed from mediocrity. You won't be pushed by management, but pulled by the curiosity of colleagues. The result is that you are going to learn more in the next year than you did in the previous five, and you'll be undertaking projects that will be written up in the trade press. Best of all, you'll get the chance to make a difference, to truly help customers and coworkers.

Who would want to be, say, a mere graphic designer or sales rep, when you could be a Warriori or Wild Brain or Angel, when you could be, in other words, a hero?

* * *

Before moving on, let's keep in mind these principles about worthy allies from inside and outside the organization:

- Be the one who is most THERE.
- Seek worthy allies and seek to be worthy of them.

PART FIVE
PROTECTING THE CIRCLES OF HELPING

- *Protect and Serve Circles of Expanding Usefulness*

75

There are two tasks of a leader, one at either end of the zone of competence. Most management is spent at the bottom end, defining acceptable behavior, trying to correct problems, enforcing policies. But the excitement comes at the upper end, inspiring new definitions of what is possible, killing the status quo.

When you embrace creative usefulness, you are operating at the highest level of management. Meanwhile, you have some employees clinging to the bottom, crying, "It's not fair! I'm doing acceptable work!" They're bureaucrats who like it at the bottom and have no intention of moving up with you. What to do with them? Doing something is important—it would be easy to look the other way—so important that we need to direct attention to protecting the circles of usefulness.

1. *You are becoming your co-workers.*

If you are the boss, you might assume that employees will become like you. True. But, at the same time, you are taking on their traits. Those around us pull upon our personalities like the planets affecting each others' orbits. You may be the biggest planet in your solar system, but your orbit is influenced by all the other orbits.

2. *If there are twelve clowns in a ring, you can jump in the middle and start reciting Shakespeare, but to the audience, you'll just be the thirteenth clown.*

— Adam Walinsky

Every person in your department defines you. The worst person especially, because that person is the embodiment of what you find acceptable. Every employee is the department. Every employee is you.

3. *A meeting moves at the pace of the slowest mind in the room.*

Take those three ideas together and you realize that allowing employees to be mediocre is not being kind or generous; it's dangerous. Never forget that there is good and bad turnover.

The best bosses know that getting the right people is 90 percent of management. Along with that knowledge comes an understanding of the need for protecting the group from those who hold it back, including those inside the group.

Todd McFarlane, creator of *Spawn* comics, puts it this way: "In an ideal world, you're an expansion team and you go out and win the World Series. Not gonna happen. As a boss you want to be loyal to the .220 hitter because he has a nice smile and tries hard, but you have to understand that HE WON'T TAKE YOU TO THE WORLD SERIES."

Once you understand the importance of every employee being admirable, it creates the necessity to hire more carefully and to reconsider employees who can't, or don't want to, keep up. This seems like a brutal Darwinian process, but when undertaken by a kindhearted person, it doesn't feel brutal; in fact, it doesn't even feel like firing—it's more like de-hiring.

A great boss assumes the best about employees—that they want to excel. That's why Roy Vallee, CEO of Avnet, has a "Two-Strike Rule." If an employee isn't first-rate, the first assumption is that something is wrong with the "fit," not the person. And so the employee is transferred to another manager. The "two strikes" part of the rule says that if someone fails twice, the company gives up. As Vallee put it, "We know that some of those people would work out on a third try, but we're not an employment agency." Notice how, even after failing in two spots, Vallee is open-minded; he simply thinks the odds are growing longer at each attempt. What I like about this approach is that it takes away the moral topspin: you don't have to work up resentment against, saying, "These people are losers," you simply say, "They have yet to find their place, and the odds are that it's somewhere else."

The reason the best managers are slow to condemn employees is that they've seen how many blossom elsewhere. One executive was about to fire a project manager. He was putting it off, trying to figure out just how and when to swing the axe, when the young man said in a staff meeting, "I've been playing around with some software and thought it might help with inventory control." Turns out that it was a breakthrough, better than anything they could buy, and so they moved him to the I.T. department, where he is a star.

Blame the fit, not the employee. If you do, the process of working with mediocre employees goes from you threatening an employee to working together to explore the best future for everyone.

THE SECRETS OF DE-HIRING

Employees should never live in fear, wondering whether or not they might be fired. Instead, they should know exactly when and why they will be fired. (And if all goes well, will either triumph or leave before it happens.)

John Opland is the sales manager for Harkness Furniture in Tacoma. He says, "I take it as a challenge to do everything to make every employee successful." And he has been challenged often, because at a prior job, he was sent all the management trainees who were floundering—a halfway house for failing employees. But, even when Opland has ended up having to ax people, they often say something like,

"Thanks for all you've done for me—I know you tried everything."

The key to the "trying everything" is involving the employee. Opland sets goals and then adds, "We're going to achieve these. What do you need from me? How do we do it? What do you suggest?"

But notice the hidden advantage: setting goals puts struggling employees in charge of their futures. And if they KNOW they are failing, and KNOW that they ultimately are going to be fired, they KNOW they need to get out and find a new job.

The best way to de-hire someone is for them to find a better job elsewhere. Bernie Palmatier, a headhunter out of Dayton, offers his clients a marvelous service. He came upon the idea in a previous career, when he was a manager who had an employee he couldn't get along with. He called a headhunter and said, "Would you recruit this employee away from me?" The headhunter did just that, then filled the job left open.

Now that he's a headhunter himself, Palmatier frequently works the same double-switch for his clients. I asked if he worried about shoving a lousy employee off on someone else. He responded by insisting that I thought too little of people. He added an example: "There was one woman, an office manager, whose boss called me and said, 'She's so abrasive, I dread going into my own office.' But I placed her with a construction company that needed people who could hold their own with some tough guys, and she was really, really good."

And then Palmatier added a sentence that should guide us all when doing some outplacing of our own: "Why destroy someone's ego? Every human being can be successful someplace." An executive who adopts that motto can increase healthy turnover and still fire fewer people.

Leadership is showing employees the future, which sometimes means showing them the door. Nearly all employees who get fired are going to end up saying, "It was the best thing to ever happen to me." So while being fired may feel like being left behind on the ice floe, it's actually the first passage to looking back in satisfaction.

At a recent meeting with a group of insurance agents, I presented some de-hiring strategies and one of the agents, Christy Chatham, recalled that she'd had a young woman working for her whose performance had declined into mediocrity. She said to that employee one day, "Are you happy?" They had a brief, frustrating conversation, without breakthroughs. However, the next morning the employee said, "Your question prompted me to rethink where I'm going with my life. I had a talk with my parents and they are going to help me go back to college full-time." And they hugged, and they cried. The former employee is still a client of that insurance agent, and they gladly report to one another their progress.

Done improperly, without the employee's best interests in mind, questions such as "Are you happy?" are just badgering an employee. If so, they can lead to anger, resentments and lawsuits. But when done with true helpfulness, de-hiring feels not at all like firing someone. You often hear people talk about "having the guts to fire someone." Firing takes guts; de-hiring takes heart.

When people hang on, doing mediocre work, they need your intelligence to help them let go and start anew. In failure is freedom.

When the Culture Does the Hiring and De-hiring

When an organization become focused on creative usefulness, the organizational "chi" begins to take over the hiring and de-hiring. For instance, the best reason to submit yourself to the rigors of interviewing with Southwest Airlines is because you have seen the energy flowing through its employees and you want to be a part of it.

Southwest's culture hires; but it also de-hires. I spoke with Donna Conover, head of Southwest's People Department, about their six-month "fire-at-will" agreement, even with union employees. How many people don't last the six months? She paused, then said, "I don't know. I don't think we've ever put together that number, but now you've got me curious. I'll find out." (Another example of the eagerness of gifted bosses to learn.) The next week she called to say, "I have it: 4.6 percent." She added, "But we don't capture why they left, so I can't tell you how many quit versus how many were asked to leave." She went on to explain that her experience led her to believe that very few were shoved out by management, although some were shoved out by the culture. She gave this: "I used to work in Reservations, and one day one of our new employees came to me and announced she was quitting. I was sorry to see her go and asked why she wanted to leave. She said, 'You want me to be happy all the time.'"

"I was unprepared for this, and it made me think. I told her, 'I'm not happy all the time. I try to be positive all the time, but I'm not happy all the time.' The employee just shrugged and said, 'Call it whatever you want, I just can't do it.'"

Create an environment obsessed with creative usefulness and the culture becomes an incentive for those with warrior spirit to join the organization, while it is an incentive for seekers of the easiest possible job to walk away.

THE NEW LOYALTY
or
GETTING DE-HIRED BY AN EMPLOYEE

Yes: The young sparrows
If you treat them tenderly
Thank you with droppings.

— Issa, Eighteenth-Century Japanese poet

During the great employee drought of the 1990s, we learned a lot about the new loyalty, and I came up with this new definition: Loyalty is the number of employees who have not yet had a better offer.

The typical response when employees leave, especially valued ones, is for them to be blamed, then forgotten. This is a mistake that gifted bosses rarely make. So your employee gets a better chance elsewhere—good for him or good for her. What is turning against former employees going to accomplish? It will make them feel free to counterattack, thereby setting off a spiral of resentments.

Permit me to tell you the story of an employee of mine who broke my heart. She was new to town, and her only experience was working in her uncle's bank. She said she wanted to do sales, despite the fact that she had no background for it. I decided to take a chance on her, and it worked. She was a marvel. I heaped new responsibilities on her, plus more training and more rewards. And then, the evening before she was to fly across the country to seal a deal with our supplier for a new product line she would be responsible for, she called and said she was quitting. I soon learned she was going to work for our only major competitor.

The competitor had offered her nearly double what I was paying, including a commission rate that was truly nonsensical: it perplexed me because I knew he would be losing money on every sale she made.

We postponed the new product line. And within days discovered that she was calling on all of our best accounts. Because she knew exactly what we offered, she knew exactly how to undercut our deal. It was a sad time, not just for the business, but for me personally; after all, I had taken a chance on her, and I'd personally taken a lot of time to train and mentor her. I thought of her as a traitor, and never spoke to her again.

Well, our company recovered—although I never did take on that new product line. But guess what happened to her? She got laid-off within three months. And then I saw all: Our competitor was able to pay her a ridiculous sum because to him it was just a temporary expense. He was buying our information and a shot at our best customers. He squeezed her like a grapefruit and then tossed her aside.

I later heard that she'd moved back home and gone back to work at the family business, her spirits broken by the hiring/firing flip-flop. It didn't do much for my spirits, either. But looking back I can see where I went wrong. Not just where she went wrong, but where I went wrong.

If I had been more open with her when she said she was leaving, maybe she would have discussed the offer and we could have figured out that it wasn't sustainable. Or, at least, if I hadn't reacted with hurt and anger, maybe she wouldn't have felt so free to go after our best customers. If nothing else, if I assumed the best and treated her as a "graduate," and remained in contact, I'm guessing she would have come back to me after a few weeks, after she discovered the real plot. And I would have welcomed her back—we could have undone the damage to our accounts, and then some. And she would have been a more loyal employee—a better employee who knew quite a lot about our competitor. And we would have added that new product line.

The point of all of this is that when you expect employees to leave, you make it less likely that they do so. And that's why the investment in lifting up an employee is not so dangerous as it seems.

The best employees are going to advance somewhere. If it isn't with you, then with someone else. But if they are learning, growing, and evolving, you've taken away much of what someone else can offer.

And if they still leave, then stay in touch—either they will realize they made a mistake, and return to you; or else they find someplace better and then you really want to stay in touch in order to figure out what you can do even better, thus maintaining the circle of helping.

*   *   *

From our discussion of de-hiring and being de-hired, we can add the following:

- Protect and serve circles of expanding usefulness.

PART SIX
EXPANDING THE CIRCLES

- *Amplify Organizational "chi":*
  Who Else Can We Help?

Upper Management and Other Customers

The least effective corporate employees see those above them in the hierarchy as The Enemy; the most successful corporate people see those above them as The Customer. Warriors don't just report to management; they charm management. What they sell is the idea that the customer is the real boss, and that the conversation is how to be more useful to the customer.

This solves one corporate mystery: Why is it that corporations say they encourage creativity and then hammer you when you present ideas? I was talking with Thomas Schmidt, a consultant from A.T. Kearney, when together we realized that to tell most bosses, "I have an idea," simply sets off the old not-invented-here alarm. When you say you have an idea, you're saying that YOU found a better way, something your boss hadn't thought. That means you're likely to be headed for the MY WAY versus YOUR WAY debate. Instead, if you say, "I'd like your opinion on whether this might help our customers," you are asking a boss to join you in an OUR PLAN discussion. As you'll recall from our discussion on charming people into giving their best, the curiosity/learning approach overcomes most natural resistance.

When dealing with their supervisors, most corporate managers seem to forget all that they learned about management. The principles are the same—the goal is to engage everyone in circles of creative usefulness, seeking allies in making OUR plan work.

You sometimes hear the expression "managing up," which is similar to what I'm describing. But because most managing-down is counterproductive, I don't suspect that most managing-up is effective, either. After all, most managers are really manipulators, and that is even more problematic going up than down. However, if you think of the work as the boss, then you aren't manipulating those around you, you are finding allies in the battle against the Dragons of Mediocrity. This means that you stop trying to convince management you are right, and you start trying to engage them in the rightness of creative usefulness. You recruit up.

Sending Up "Chi"

Bob Nelson, the author of the important and practical book, *1001 Ways to Reward Employees*, recently completed his Ph.D. In his dissertation he studied what caused managers to use or not use rewards and recognition. He discovered many factors correlated with frequent use of "non-monetary recognition" including the following:
- "My employees like working for me because I recognize them when they do good work," and
- "I've been thanked and acknowledged for the job I do by my employees."

On the other end of the spectrum, the items associated with low use of non-monetary recognition" included this:
- "My employees do not value the recognition I have provided to them in the past."

It seems so fundamental, yet few employees realize that they are part of circles of helping, and that they need to do their part to keep the mojo flowing. The karma in organizations doesn't just flow down; it circles around the organization and anyone in the circle has the choice to either block the flow of energy or reinforce it. There's an Irish supermarket chain where all the employees wear miniature boomerangs on their lapels. The goal is to remind everyone "whatever you send out comes back to you."

Once you understand the circularity of organizational energy, and if you accept that you are one of many people competing for the resources of the organization, you realize that you seek to earn those resources by being their "highest and best use"— the most profitable, most intriguing, most energizing, most innovative, most helpful. Just as in selling to customers, you sell to management with creative usefulness.

What management actions create blockages in the energy flow? Resentments, distrust, and other conflicts. One study of managers (as reported in *Primal Leadership*) found that the most common source of conflict was "inept criticism." Sadly, most management is criticism, and most criticism is inept. In fact, we could make a case that ALL criticism is inept—it is a failure of hiring or organizing or inspiring. If you are a manager, your goal should be to spend your time praising, not criticizing.

Try this experiment: Feel free to offer any one criticism, just as soon as you've given a thousand compliments. Such an approach doesn't mean you can't help someone learn or improve; it's just that criticism rarely leads to either learning or improvement. Picture a situation in which someone has asked you to review a report he or she has written. Imagine the difference between saying, "The ending is weak" versus "As I read the ending, I kept thinking about that terrific summary on your last report. Is there some way to get that power into this one?" This is not just management by asking questions, it is management by compliments, by calling to strengths.

But even if we agree that criticism doesn't work, that doesn't mean you won't get plenty of it directed at you. If you are managed, then you should steel yourself against the inevitability of (inept) criticism. As with our discussion of shyness and "organizations suck," awareness of the inevitability of criticism is itself the best defense.

The Art of Being Criticizable

During a Q&A session at a conference, Thomas Krens, director of the Guggenheim Museums, was asked why he had repeated himself by going back to Frank Gehry as architect for the new Guggenheim in New York City. (Gehry had also done the celebrated Guggenheim in Bilbao, Spain.) Krens answered, "You can criticize him."

This seemed to be a thin rationale, and I sat down with him after his speech for a remarkable visit. First off, I argued that any architect would cooperate when offered a chance like the Guggenheim. After all, Krens's goal for the building was stunning: "Something better than [the cathedral at] Chartres, better than Sydney [Opera House]." Talk about a "hero shot"—surely any architect would cooperate. "No," he explained, "with most architects, you criticize them and you get in a fight. With Gehry, if you don't like it, he's happy to tear it up."

I wondered aloud if it is a lack of vanity that makes Gehry so agreeable. Krens laughed, saying, "He has a bigger ego than any architect I know. He knows he's a genius. But he also knows that he's so good that if he does it over, with more information, it will be even better."

I hope you are a genius. If so, it would become you to be a genius you can criticize.

*   *   *

If you are ready to win over your boss with the Zen of being criticizable, then you should meet Brad Harper of Trigon Executive Assessment. Corporations hire him to work with employees who range from having been singled out for rapid advancement to those who are in danger of being axed. As for the latter, he makes them understand that a willingness to alter their behavior is only the start; the larger task is to get others to notice the change.

Say that Harper is called in to work with an employee who is quite valuable, but who has a temper that is undermining his work. Harper will have him go to people important to his career and say something like this: "I want to work on my relationships, and I know that people find me abrasive. What two or three ideas do you have for me?" Then comes what Harper calls the two most critical steps in the process: "One, Shut your mouth. Two, then say 'thank you.'"

Notice what happens to perceptions of our angry man. Say he goes three months without exploding and then blows up. If he hasn't involved others in his changing, they will merely find the outburst more evidence that he "has a problem." But, if he's involved others, they are likely to think, "It's been months," and to offer encouragement when he next asks for feedback.

Harper uses a study by Kilty, Goldsmith & Co. that shows the power of asking for feedback (whether or not you get it). They correlated the perceived increase in effectiveness of managers with feedback. Here is the percentage of managers given the highest possible effectiveness rating, alongside the extent of feedback they sought:

Feedback Sought	% Given Highest Rating
Little	4%
Some	7%
Frequent	21%
Constant	55%

Harper says, in his experience, even if the amount of actual change were held constant, the perceived change would soar with the number of requests for feedback.

If you treat criticism from a boss as you would as from a customer, as important feedback, then you have a chance of learning instead of arguing or rationalizing. As Oscar Wilde once said, a person should know "the precise psychological moment to say nothing."

Customer "Chi"

Speaking of learning from customers, Mike Gersten of Intrinsic Technologies, an IT consulting firm, had an occasion when his team lost a project they really wanted—an unusual occurrence for them, not having happened for more than two years. Their first reaction was hurt and anger, saying of the lost client, "THEY made a mistake and THEY'LL end up regretting the decision." Then, Gersten said, "We realized it was OUR fault. They needed the lowest cost solution, not the one we thought was best." Gersten had the executive maturity to realize that because he had failed to understand the client's needs, he didn't deserve the assignment.

But that doesn't mean you expect customers to provide solutions, or even to know what they want. Just start with their problems and "How can we help?" will make sense. For example, you could do a hundred focus groups on office furniture and not have a customer say, "I want a chair made out of something like pantyhose material." But once Chadwick and Stumpf found the study that showed that heat was as big a problem as pressure, the problem suggested the solution. That's why wise executives don't avoid problems; they seek them out. The goal isn't to eliminate problems but to move up to better ones, like a figure skater moving up to better and better competitions.

Before long, you and your employees will take pride in seeking out bigger and better problems, moving beyond the competition to an understanding that The Real Competition is always laying to rest your former status quo.

Price or The Emotions of Money

Once you start to see your work as circles of usefulness and flows of energy, you have to assess whom to allow into each circle. Not everyone will send back what you send out. While most people will eagerly join you for a ride up the spiral of usefulness, there are others who will suck your staff's energy into a Black Hole of gloom.

Sitting through a presentation by a professor droning on about how price-sensitive "switchers" were not really worth the trouble as customers, a fellow member of the audience, Rob Dalton, the owner of a company that sells industrial steam cleaning equipment, leaned over and said, "What he's saying is a mooch is a mooch is a mooch. The same guy who beats you up on price, is the same guy who is going to complain, and is the same guy who is going to alienate your employees."

You give in on price and get a hard time. Mooches don't just hammer down costs, they hammer down your spirit. You can't soar and niggle at the same time.

Norm Stoehr, who runs Inner Circle (a company out of Minneapolis that creates advisory boards in which business owners meet and exchange ideas) says, "If you offer 'the highest quality and the best service at a competitive price,' people won't trust you." They won't trust you because they know, consciously or unconsciously, that it isn't true.

Stoehr also tells the story of a company out of Minneapolis that makes horse blankets—ones they believe to be the best in the world. Their strategy was to sell these quality blankets at about $65, a price similar to that of competitors.

The company wanted to increase its sales, and Stoehr's solution was to increase prices. The owner objected, saying, "We make a fair profit now." But, Stoehr explained, the key market is Arabian horse owners, mostly people who are wealthy and who want the best, who are looking to buy "a blanket that is worthy of the steed." So the company increased the price to $250, and sales went up—not just dollar sales, but unit sales, as well.

So what's going on here? You try to discount and merely get trouble—is it bad karma? Sponge voodoo? Mooch juju?

The answer is this: Price isn't just money; it's emotion. Price is the start of a relationship. If you cut prices to get business, you don't just give up money, you give up respect as well—after all, you just proved that your "regular price" was a kind of lie. You have proven that your customers have to keep an eye on you, keep after you, that you can't be trusted. In other words, you start by giving in on price and you've already begun giving up.

Who Else Can We Help?

The circles of energy include customers and employees, and also suppliers. As you create a place fit for heroes within your offices, you can gain karma by creating the same culture with suppliers. And the first thing to realize is that a relationship with suppliers is a lot more than price.

The lowest possible price you can negotiate with a supplier is what economists call "the indifference point"—that is, the point at which the supplier shrugs and says, "At this price, I don't really care if I sell or not." So, your reward for being a hard negotiator can be having soft suppliers, ones who don't really care about your business.

Kip Tindell of The Container Store insists that his relatively small chain often gets better prices than the giants, like Target or Wal-Mart. He says, "Somebody is going to get the best price, and it's not usually the one who buys the most; it's the one with the best relationship."

And how do you get that relationship in which someone gives you a great price and still cares about your business? In Tindell's case it's knowing the supplier's needs—for instance, knowing a supplier's slow time of year and timing orders to correspond. And it's knowing that seemingly small matters, like paying all invoices within 30 days, can mean a lot. (I recently met a man who does small engine repair, who told me that he had handled the local work for one of the big discount chains. But they took 60 or 90 days to pay, and they wouldn't return his calls. So he switched to another chain, which paid him weekly and "they return calls within 10 minutes." Of course you get a lot fewer calls about invoices when you pay bills weekly, so it may actually decrease their costs.)

Tindell's reward for such concern isn't just getting the lowest prices. Those relationships also mean that suppliers come with prototypes, giving the chain a hand in the design. "We get good products first, and often an exclusive," Tindell explains, "and we don't have to have an R&D department—our suppliers do that for us."

And one other thing—Tindell loves to work with small suppliers, including start-ups, and takes pride in often being the first to take a chance on a small manufacturer. He says, "I have often heard manufacturers say, "We wouldn't be in business today if it weren't for The Container Store." Now that's corporate karma.

How to start?

1. **The Invitation**. Go to your suppliers and ask them how you can help them. This seems backward—they should be asking you how they can help. But if you just sit back, demanding lower prices, you are just one of many customers, one of the

commoners: the enemy.

If you take the time to know your suppliers, you might be able to say something like this: "I know that you've been wanting to try some new techniques. I have some suggestions that fit. Why don't we try it, and when we're done, we can write it up for the trade press." In other words, let's be heroes together.

2. **The Reward**. Next, you might want to consider creating awards for your suppliers. Rex Johnson reflecting on his time at Baxter Credit Union, described how he started annual Business Partner Days, which were meetings with suppliers designed to find ways to expand usefulness. One time he met with the company who supplied the specialty checks the credit union sold to its members, and they agreed to create a ranking for how successful the branches were in selling upgraded checks, as well as publishing a newsletter offering marketing suggestions. The two companies were helping each other sell more. (By the way, Johnson added that the check provider made the agreed-upon efforts for only about six months, then stopped. So Johnson replaced that supplier. I must not forget that these are circles of helping, not circles of promises.)

The Baxter Credit Union also began procedures to evaluate suppliers, including how promptly they handled problems, how often they visited headquarters and the branches and so on. During the Partner Days, the credit union presented awards for the top rated suppliers, giving the winners a crystal sculpture of an eagle.

Although these awards may seem like a way to attract more helpfulness to the Baxter Credit Union, it was also helpful to the winners. Because the awards were based on a series of evaluations, the awards came to have meaning in the industry, like a Baldrige Award. So the winners would use their awards to attract more business. All of which is starting to sound like a trip around some circles of creative usefulness.

3. **The Education**. Brighton Accessories, a $100+ million manufacturer of watches and handbags, has set itself apart from other companies by saying "no" to being the supplier to some of the country's largest accounts.

   The founder, Jerry Kohl, started out running a specialty store and now sells to gift shops and other small retailers, avoiding the large chains. Kohl's own experience suggested that specialty retailers were ignored or under-served by most vendors. Not Brighton. Salespeople visit all retail accounts at least once a month. Plus, once a year, the top retailers are invited to visit the company for "Brighton Week," a series of all-day workshops. Brighton spends nearly a million dollars to host several hundred retailers with the goal of teach-the-teachers, to give the retailers sufficient knowledge and enthusiasm that they pass on to customers. The company thrives because it is so helpful to the companies that sell its goods.

So we see that the search for new circles of energy moves up and down the supply chain—perhaps it would be good to think of that chain as being made of circles of creative usefulness.

We also see the circles moving together, wheels within wheels. In every relationship—customers, employees, upper management, suppliers—the goal is to expand usefulness and thereby release the emotional energy of caring and the playfulness of curiosity.

                    *   *   *

   From our review of issues of dealing with upper management, suppliers and customers, we can appreciate this Principle.

• Amplify organizational "chi": Who else can we help?

PART SEVEN
FINAL THOUGHTS

- *Create Wealths*

The company's president sighed. He'd just gotten new numbers and, well, a sigh summed them up. He'd employed all his old management tricks, and yet the company would not respond. He'd redoubled his efforts: written goals, policies, and missions; he was everywhere, herding the organization. Still, most employees were not committed; their only creativity seemed to arise out of figuring out how to do as little as possible. What was wrong with them?

Desperate to figure it out, he decided that his newest initiative would be an open-door policy. Making a show of it, he had his office door taken off its hinges and turned into a coffee table that was placed in front of the couch in his office.

Was this open-door effort the one to finally bring ·he organization together? With another boss this might have been a playful and effective gesture, but, in this case, the employees just sighed and said, "I wish he'd go in his office, lock the door, and never come out. Maybe then we could get some work done."

What the president failed to understand was that employees always have a choice: They can either do their jobs or do their best. You can't write enough policies to force people to do their best. In fact, you can't even coerce yourself into doing your best, at least not for very long—your brain must be charmed into being involved and fully utilized. What the president couldn't teach those who worked for him, because he didn't know it himself, is the Zen of problems. Wise leaders and high achievers come to understand that they can't hope to eliminate problems—and wouldn't want to—but rather aspire to a better class of opponent, one that charms the mind. Where to find such a worthy opponent?

• THINK LIKE A HERO (Who can I help today?)
• WORK LIKE AN ARTIST (What else can we try?)

When curiosity and usefulness come together, the effect is like the Samurai warrior calling for a worthy opponent.

Here are two final examples of how Laughing Warriors use creative usefulness to kill the status quo.

THE SCIENTIST

Talk about a worthy opponent: Brian Druker discovered a cure for cancer. (A Novartis drug called Gleevec has reversed a form of leukemia known as CML, and it has kept it reversed for four years and counting.)

Druker started in oncology, where he would sit with his patients, many of them doomed, and talk about their lives. He said, simply, "I've always thought that the greatest gift is time, and I was willing to take some time to ask about their lives."

Whenever one of those lives ended, he would send a note to the family that said some version of this: "I will remember what we couldn't do for your mother. This will motivate me as I enter my lab career, so maybe some day we can have more to offer."

As he went to his lab career, he was not thinking he was going to find a cure for cancer, but asking himself, "Where could I make the greatest contribution?" He decided to study gene therapies: "I was very undirected, wanting to learn as much as I could and see where it would take me." Where it took him was to where he could say, "I knew cancer backwards and forward. I knew this enzyme backwards and forward. It became absolutely clear what I should do."

Druker receives more notes than he sends these days. He had one from one of his first participants in the clinical trials, and it moved him for its simplicity. As he read it, his voice strained to maintain the coolness of the scientist: "Thank you for the extra time with my family."

THE EXECUTIVE

Pete Rahn was a small town insurance agent until he was selected to be the head of the highway department for New Mexico. He had no engineering degree, and his knowledge of highways came from inside the car, not out, which turned out to be a huge advantage—he couldn't tell the staff how to build highways better or faster, but he could ask questions. Perhaps the most important of these was why New Mexico's highways were among the worst in the nation. So he met with employees at every level, asking what was holding them back.

As an outsider, Rahn could see what insiders could not. For example, because much of the money for highways comes from the federal government, and one of the biggest obstacles to building roads is the federal bureaucracy, he asked the federal representative assigned to New Mexico, Rueben Thomas, to join his staff meetings, even the planning sessions and retreats.

Rahn explained, "The conventional thinking was 'They spy on us. They police us. They try to catch us doing something wrong.'" With Thomas inside, the result was a partnership so effective that Washington called Thomas to ask why he hadn't been issuing "pink slips" for violations. He gleefully described what transpired next: "I told them that I wasn't writing up violations because I was now heading off problems before they started. Still, they pressured me. Finally, I called up Pete and said, 'Do you have something I could pink slip?'"

How is it working out? One example is the rebuilding the intersection of Interstates 40 and 25 in Albuquerque. A similar project will take five years in Texas and eight years in Virginia. Rahn's department did it in 23 months. New Mexico's highways are now among the best in the country, and engineers fly in from around the country to study what went right in an agency that was run by a man with no engineering background.

These are two examples of doing the impossible, two examples of the effervescence that arises from mixing creativity with the fundamental human desire to be useful.

Notice the emphasis on learning. Rahn met with employees at every level, asking them what stood between them and achievement. And then we have that telling sentence of Druker's: "I was very undirected, wanting to learn as much as I could and see where it would take me."

See where it would take me. High achievers are explorers. They aren't passive recipients of knowledge; rather, by learning from every direction, they see connections opening up: Achievement is the ability to learn more than you are taught. It is the relentlessness of Gandhi curiosity, and it has the power to turn adversaries into allies against a common foe—the status quo.

CREATING WEALTHS

The people we've met in this book understand the unseen energies of organizational "chi." They know we aren't rational beings—we are emotional beings pretending to be rational. And while we must satisfy the rational mind, our real goal is to charm the emotional one.

Then, if we understand that our hardwiring makes us ill-suited for organization success, we can stop trying to fix organizations, and start trying to charm them. While we can't eliminate the dark side of our natures, we can grow preoccupied with our better selves. This is how Warriors of Usefulness defeat the Dragons, with the energy that arises from aligning the best of self-interest with the best of organizational effectiveness.

While business is a game of numbers, real achievement is measured in infinite, emotional wealths: friendship, usefulness, helping, laughter, learning. Or, said another way, The one who dies with the most joys wins.

* * *

With this, we add the final entry in The Code of The Laughing Warrior:

- *Create wealths.*

CONCLUSION

• *The Code of The Laughing Warrior*

As you prepare for the inevitable encounters with the Dragons in your realm, go into battle armed with this guide:

**The Code of
The Laughing Warrior**
(The Way of Creative Usefulness)

- Think like a hero: Who can I help today?

- Work like an artist: What else can we try?

- Refuse to be ordinary: Pursue excellence and kill it.

- Celebrate, but take no credit.

- Accept that organizations call forth the worst in human nature and be liberated by that knowledge.

- Looking through "eyes that encourage," spot the gifts of others and hold them up for all to admire.

- Practice Gandhi curiosity—experiments never fail.

- Be the one most THERE.

- Seek out worthy allies and earn their allegiance.

- Protect and serve circles of expanding usefulness.

- Amplify organizational "chi": Who ELSE can we help?

- Create wealths.

Finally, as promised, we end by returning to the story of the young merchant who'd been given three days to either become an enlightened leader or to die. You'll recall that he'd met a wise executive who'd told him, "If you're not learning, you're not doing it right," and later, "If you're not laughing, you're not doing it right." He'd studied but had made no progress, till the day before the one on which he was to die. Here is what he discovered:

After hearing that I had just three days, I spent the first of those days frantically seeking enlightenment. On the second day, I realized it was pointless, and simply gave up, admitting that I could no longer hope to remake the people around me. Instead, I went to those who worked with me and asked for their help. I explained that because I wouldn't be there to supervise them, I would allot assignments based on their special gifts, and seek to create situations where those talents would need no supervision.

Together we started making plans, and as they anticipated what they might accomplish, I watched the energy boil in their eyes. Suddenly they were eager to offer help, not just take it. I could see the dormant warrior spirit rise in them, could feel their eagerness to take up the sword of creative usefulness and do battle with the existing standards of excellence.

As for me, oh, how I yearned to be there, to be part of it. I craved this new curiosity. I ached for the satisfaction of being useful in new and clever ways. I daydreamed of the friendships that would arise and longed to live them.

Then, as my workers excitedly talked on, I realized that I was learning about what mattered most: how to call to the best in people instead of looking for the worst in them. And that's when I started laughing at what a fool I'd been. They looked at me, amazed. I found more humor in their surprised gazes and laughed on. That's when, at that exact moment, I knew I was learning and laughing—I knew that, at last, I was doing it right.

A NOTE TO THE READER

If you decide to become a Laughing Warrior, please visit www.dauten.com. There, you can print out free copies of THE CODE OF THE LAUGHING WARRIOR to post in your workplace. You can also find information on related books and my seminars on "How to Enjoy Killing the Status Quo."

Further, if you'd like to be part of group of managers, executives and entrepreneurs who come together to help each other think like heroes and work like artists, please visit www.InnovatorsLab.com.

ACKNOWLEDGEMENTS

I'd like to thank all of the people who inspired this book and gave of their time to put up with my questions. Except where stated otherwise, the stories and examples in this book are from personal interviews.

I am further indebted to those who helped me capture and put on paper the wisdom of Laughing Warriors. I'd like to thank Jim Fickess, Paula Wigboldy, Janiene Schultz, Dan Peitzmeyer, Bobette Gorden, Jeff Figler, Richard Gooding, Joel Dauten, John Genzale, Sandy Dauten, Kirsten Paley, Bethany Murray, Caleb Naugle, Don Schweiker, Jeff Murphy, Rick Hamada, Jason Meyer, Doug Ducey, Jim Camp, Mark Cashion, Janet Traylor, and John Ball.

APPENDIX

REVELATIONS TO SUPPORT
THE CODE OF THE LAUGHING WARRIOR

REVELATION #1
We are emotional beings pretending to be rational.

REVELATION #2
If you focus on customers' emotions—on making sure they feel helped, and on making them laugh and smile—your attitude will take care of itself. Plus, when you're helping, you don't burn energy, you manufacture it.

REVELATION #3
Never forget that you only truly succeed by making yourself into a person worthy of success.

REVELATION #4
The fiercest competitors are Warriors of Usefulness, who come armed with curiosity, experimentation, and the joy of creative helpfulness.

REVELATION #5
The Big Bang Theory of Business: The history of success is the story of expanding usefulness.

REVELATION #6
Different isn't always better, but better is always different.

REVELATION #7

Some of the things you do NOT need to start experimenting: leadership, management, inspiration, teams, budgets, permission, help, ideas.

REVELATION #8

REFUSE TO BE ORDINARY.

Most people are daunted by creativity; instead, make a decision to stop being ordinary and you end up at the same place faster and easier.

REVELATION #9

EXPERIMENTS NEVER FAIL.

The most important determinant of innovation is the willingness to experiment.

REVELATION #10

People hate to change but love to experiment.

REVELATIONS #11

Learning and usefulness intersect into Circles of Usefulness—you help by learning and learn by helping. Count the day lost when the two don't come together for you.

REVELATION #12

Hierarchy is forever.

— Nigel Nicholson

REVELATION #13

Just as certainly as spiders are born to weave webs, so we are genetically predisposed to create environments of which we want no part. In other words, it is natural that organizations tend to suck.

REVELATION #14

Once you start to accept the idea that people are partly "hardwired," then you can stop blaming them and stop trying to change them; rather, you start finding the right use for their brain "equipment."

REVELATION #15

The popular management advice, "Hire good people and get out of their way" is flawed. Without meaning to, most employees, even good ones, opt for the safety of mediocrity. Being exceptional is unnatural. The role of leadership is to save us from our programming—not to get out of the way, but to remind us of the way.

REVELATION #16

The real heroes in any organization are the ones who refuse to be ordinary, who refuse to give into bureaucracy and to the "programming" that create the relentless pull of mediocrity.

REVELATION #17

As executives are promoted, they tend to say more and hear less. They fall into the trap of thinking that they are paid to make decisions—to make pronouncements and give speeches. No. They succeed by finding people who make the decisions obvious. They succeed by listening, not speaking. The best succeed with their ears.

REVELATION #18

There's nothing less impressive than trying to be impressive. Great minds dwell not on what they know, but what they don't. After all, what is curiosity but ignorance embraced?

REVELATION #19

People will exercise great effort and creativity to make OUR plan work; and sometimes expend just as much effort and creativity to make YOUR plan fail.

— Bob Klas, CEO of TapeMark

REVELATION #20

Empty hands; closed mind.

REVELATION #21

If you aren't working on projects that will land you on the cover of your trade magazine, then you don't deserve the best employees.

REVELATION #22

An experiment is nonpassive learning; it's aggressive curiosity; it's Gandhi curiosity. A plan is an edict—an experiment is an adventure.

REVELATION #23

This is all it takes: somebody whose eyes encourage, whose attitude is eager and unreserved.

— Eknath Easwaran

REVELATION #24

He talked about my strengths. He reminded me how good I was.

— Peter Sampras describing how Tim Gullickson made him a great player

REVELATION #25

Catch a glimpse of someone's gift and hold it up for them to admire.

REVELATION #26

Criticism makes people smaller—defensive, cautious, striving to be invisible. Praise makes people larger—they rise and open like a flower going to the light.

REVELATION #27

You don't have to be the one who works the most hours, just the one who is most there during the hours you work. Come to work and put your heart on the table.

— James Evans, former CEO of Best Western Hotels

REVELATION #28

It is wise to assume that the unemployment rate among the top one percent of talent is always hovering just above zero. Such stars rarely walk in and ask for a job; they have to be spotted and courted.

REVELATION #29

Here is the most important advice on hiring I can give you: See the work, not just the person. SEE THE WORK with your own eyes, or at least talk to those who have seen it, which is to see it through the eyes of others. SEE THE WORK. SEE THE WORK.

REVELATION #30

Judge not, because you aren't very good at it. (The best people match no stereotype because being exceptional is the opposite of being stereotypical.)

REVELATION #30

Ugly people are a bargain.

REVELATION #31

The person you interview is never the person you hire.

REVELATION #32

The job market is the used car lot of employment.

REVELATION #33

Installing a lie detector in your office would make you a worse manager, not better. The greater danger comes not from those who seek to lie to you, but from those who have lied to themselves.

REVELATION #34

If the people you'd love to hire were the sort to leap at a 10 percent increase in pay, they wouldn't be people you'd love to hire.

REVELATION #35

You can't offer big talent a little bribe; you have to offer either a big bribe or a big chance. The best employees know they will be well compensated, so the key decision criteria go beyond money—they want to take the stage, to show off, to make a difference, to be heroes.

REVELATION #36

Hiring is circular helping—the goal is to find the person who will contribute the most AND benefit the most.

REVELATION #37

Here is the wisdom of the best bosses: Organizations thrive when employees choose to bestow the gift of excellence upon them.

REVELATION #38

While many executives can tell you at what percent of capacity of their plants, none can tell you the percent of capacity at which their employees' brains operate; after all, creativity and initiative are unlimited resources.

REVELATION #39

To a true leader, there are no sweeter words to hear than "Follow me."

REVELATION #40

The best people understand that you can't be successful without sacrifice. The best never complain about sacrifices—they're proud of them.

— Lou Holtz

REVELATION #41

While many corporate managers now think of themselves as "coaches," the best coaches have always thought of themselves as teachers. Perhaps it would be wise to eliminate the intermediate step; after all, the most accomplished entrepreneurs, executives and salespeople are the most effective educators.

REVELATION #42

They knew they'd get more than just basketball.

— John Wooden explaining his recruiting at UCLA.

REVELATION #43

You are becoming your co-workers.

REVELATION #44

If there are twelve clowns in a ring, you can jump in the middle and start reciting Shakespeare, but to the audience, you'll just be the thirteenth clown.

— Adam Walinsky

REVELATION #45

A meeting moves at the pace of the slowest mind in the room.

REVELATION #46

Allowing employees to be mediocre is not being kind or generous; it's dangerous. Never forget that there is good and bad turnover.

REVELATION #47

Employees should never live in fear, wondering whether or not they might be fired. Instead, they should know they will be fired. (And, if all goes well, will either triumph or leave before it happens.)

REVELATION #48

Leadership is showing employees the future, which sometimes means showing them the door. Nearly all employees who get fired are going to end up saying, "It was the best thing to ever happen to me." So, while being fired may feel like being left behind on the ice floe, it's actually the first passage to looking back in satisfaction.

REVELATION #49

When done with true helpfulness, de-hiring feels not at all like firing someone. You often hear people talk about "having the guts to fire someone." Firing takes guts; de-hiring takes heart.

REVELATION #50

When people hang on, doing mediocre work, they need your intelligence to help them let go and start anew. In failure is freedom.

REVELATION #51

Yes: The young sparrows
If you treat them tenderly
Thank you with droppings.

— Issa, Eighteenth-Century Japanese poet

REVELATION #52

Loyalty is the number of employees who have not yet had a better offer.

REVELATION #53

The best employees are going to advance somewhere. If it isn't with you, then with someone else. But if they know they are learning, growing, and evolving working with you, you've taken away much of what someone else can offer.

REVELATION #54

The karma in organizations doesn't just flow down, it circles around the organization, and anyone in the circle can block the flow of energy or reinforce it.

REVELATION #55

The most successful corporate employees don't just report to management, they sell to management. What they sell is the idea that the customer is the real boss.

REVELATION #57

You can criticize him.

> — Thomas Krens, Director of the Guggenheim Museums, explaining why he had repeated himself by going back to Frank Gehry as architect for the new Guggenheim in New York City

REVELATION #58

A mooch is a mooch is a mooch. The same guy who beats you up on price is the same guy who is going to complain and is the same guy who is going to alienate your employees.

> — Rob Dalton, entrepreneur

REVELATION #59

Price isn't just money. Price is the start of a relationship. You cut prices to get business and you don't just give up money, you give up respect as well—after all, you just proved that your "regular price" was a kind of lie.

REVELATION #60

The lowest possible price you can negotiate with a supplier is what economists call "the indifference point"—that is, the point at which the supplier shrugs and says, "At this price I don't really care if I sell or not." So, your reward for being a hard negotiator can be having soft suppliers, ones who don't really care about your business.

REVELATION #61

The search for new circles of energy moves up and down the supply chain—perhaps it would be good to think of that "chain" as being made of circles of creative usefulness.

REVELATION #62

In every relationship—customers, employees, upper management, suppliers— the goal is to expand usefulness and thereby release the emotional energy of caring and the playfulness of curiosity. When we bring caring and curiosity together, we earn the wealths of friendship—learning, laughter, and love.